An Exposition of the Gospel of John

A Journey through JOHN

John 6–8

A New Testament Commentary Series

Dr. Stuart M. Guthrie

First edition

ISBN: 978-1-959478-06-5 (Paperback)
ISBN: 978-1-959478-07-2 (Hard Cover)
ISBN: 978-1-959478-08-9 (Ebook)

DEDICATION

I would like to dedicate this book to the many professors at Columbia International University who took time with me and taught me the tools I needed to be an effective pastor. I am truly grateful for these men who shaped my life early in my faith.

I would like to thank Dr. Michael Fiorello for his friendship and for teaching me Greek when I didn't want to learn it. For your one-on-one investment in me, not only as a student, but as a friend even today—thank you, doc. Thank you, Dr. John Crutchfield, for your countless hours of helping me to better understand and apply hermeneutics weekly; and of course, for those classes in OT survey that were so engaging and helpful! To my dear friend, Dr. Andre Rodgers, thank you for seeing in me what the Lord had not revealed to me at the time. You helped me to see my calling as a pastor, preacher, and student, and you will always be dear to my heart. To Dr. Kevin McWilliams, your classes were so helpful in applying the Word of God and challenging me in my faith.

To all the staff of CIU and Dr. Bill Jones, thanks for always being a great example to follow. I am enduringly grateful. CIU gave me a greater ability to study and preach the Word of God, and to know Christ and make Christ known—for that, I am forever thankful.

TABLE OF CONTENTS

PREFACE

John's Gospel has been transformational in the lives of so many. It has been said that the book of John is "shallow enough for a child to swim in, and yet deep enough for an elephant to drown in."

In writing this book, I have tried to provide a helpful tool for your Christian walk by encouraging you through the book of John, verse by verse and chapter by chapter. It has been my intention to balance the writing in this book so that the most basic reader can understand its content and yet also offer something the pastor can glean from in his weekly studies.

This five-book commentary series is applicational, expositional, and devotional. This volume is intended to meet you wherever you may be in your walk with the Lord. *A Journey through John* can be a helpful tool as you do your daily Bible reading, prepare to teach Sunday school classes, or sit down as a family for devotional time.

This commentary series is designed with gospel clarity and brings an opportunity for the reader not just to receive information but to experience the transforming power of the gospel. This book will make a great gift for your family, friends, and coworkers who are seeking and interested in the things of God. I pray that you will find this commentary on the Gospel of John a helpful tool as you journey through John.

CHAPTER 1

THE FEEDING OF THE 5,000
John 6:1–15

As we begin our examination of the sixth chapter of John's Gospel, we must remember that even though we are transitioning our focus away from the deity of Christ, He is still all deity! By working miracles, He is still proving that He is God! But the focus is not on deity; rather, it is on the miracles themselves. And if we zoom in a little closer, past the miracles, there is an even greater lesson we can apply to our lives. The overarching lesson is this: men are like the gods they serve.

We all live our lives based on what or Who we worship. A weak view of God results in a weak life lived for Him, because "We conduct ourselves according to the concept of the God to whom we bow," the One whom we worship.[1] Who we worship and what we think about the one we worship determines how we live and function, how we face hard times, and how we stand in this life.

Every believer should have a big view of God, and the Bible is filled with examples of people who had this perspective.

For instance, David had a big view of God when he stood before the giant, Goliath, who stood nearly ten feet tall. Remember what Goliath said to David and, more importantly, how David replied?

1 Samuel 17:44–45
44 The Philistine also said to David, "Come to me, and I will give your flesh to the birds of the sky and the beasts of the field." 45 Then David said to the Philistine, "You come to me with a sword, a spear, and a javelin, but I come to you in the name of the Lord of hosts, the God of the armies of Israel, whom you have taunted."

Clearly David had a big view of God!

Or how about King Asa, whose army of Judah was outnumbered by more than two to one as he faced the Ethiopians?

---

[1] R. Kent Hughes, *John: That You May Believe*, Preaching the Word (Wheaton, IL: Crossway, 2014), 193.

2 Chronicles 14:10–11
10 So Asa went out to meet him, and they drew up in battle formation in the Valley of Zephathah at Mareshah. 11 Then Asa called to the LORD his God and said, "LORD, there is no one besides You to help in the battle between the powerful and those who have no strength; help us, LORD our God, for we trust in You, and in Your name have come against this multitude. LORD, You are our God; do not let man prevail against You."

Like David, Asa had a big view of God!

And we are like the gods we serve. John 6 is going to point again to the reality that Jesus is the Christ, the Son of God. And not only that, but He, Christ, God in the flesh, is all-powerful. Jesus is going to teach His disciples a great lesson that will teach us a great lesson, as well. So let's look at our text, John 6:1–15.

This portion of Scripture is powerful, because it contains an account of a powerful miracle. This miracle is included in all four of the Gospels (Matt 14, Mark 6, Luke 9, and John 6). In fact, aside from the Resurrection, it's the only miracle that is mentioned in all four Gospels. Maybe that's because it's the biggest miracle yet, affecting at least 5,000 people (and perhaps as many as 25,000, including women and children). Whatever the number, there were at least 5,000 witnesses to this miracle! It is the highlight of Jesus' public ministry in Galilee, and it made such an impact on the people, as we will see, that they try to make Him king by force.

The ruler of Judea at the time was Herod Antipas. He was the son of Herod the Great, the king who was visited by the Magi and became furious when they tricked him. In his rage he gave orders to kill all of the boys in Bethlehem and its vicinity who were two years old and younger, in accordance with what he had learned from the Magi (Matt 2:16). He wanted this child, Jesus, killed! And now, during the reign of one of the sons of this evil despot, the crowd is trying to make Jesus king.

So it makes sense that after this miracle we begin to see a transition from Jesus' public ministry to a more private ministry to His disciples and smaller groups. Jesus isn't scared, but He knows His time hasn't yet come.

In light of this, there are three things we need to see as we approach this text. First, we see the problem among the crowd. Second, we see the solution among the crowd. And finally, we see the result among the crowd.

Let's begin by looking at the context of what's happening in John 6.

John 6:1
1 After these things Jesus went away to the other side of the Sea of Galilee (or Tiberias).

Here we have to ask the question, after what things? The simple answer is that "these things" refer to Jesus' encounter with the religious leaders at the end of chapter 5, when the Lord testifies about His deity.

After this encounter, He went away to the other side of the sea. But the other Gospels can help to fill in any gaps so that we can really learn and understand the timeline of what is taking place here.

Recall that in John 5 we are given a time frame for when Jesus went up to Jerusalem.

John 5:1
1 After these things there was a feast of the Jews, and Jesus went up to Jerusalem.

We are not totally certain about which feast it was, but if it was the Feast of the Tabernacles it means that about six months elapsed between the two chapters. If it was the Passover, then a whole year had passed. Either way, when John says, "After these things Jesus went away to the other side of the Sea of Galilee (or Tiberias)," a great deal of time had passed and much work had been done.

This may also help explain why there were so many followers when they crossed over to the other side of the lake—Jesus had been healing, teaching, and proclaiming the Kingdom of God for at least six months and perhaps as long as a year. And so the text continues…

John 6:2
2 A large crowd was following Him, because they were watching the signs which He was performing on those who were sick.

Jesus' ministry is a major public ministry by now. Mark 6:14–16 confirms this, telling us that,

14 And King Herod heard of it, for His name had become well known; and people were saying, "John the Baptist has risen from the dead, and that is why these miraculous powers are at work in Him." 15 But others were saying, "He is Elijah." And others were saying, "He is a prophet, like one of the prophets of old." 16 But when Herod heard of it, he kept saying, "John, whom I beheaded, has risen!"

John the Baptist has been killed by this point. The crowd has discovered Jesus, and they are following Him by foot around the lake as He and His disciples travel by boat. It seems they are not seeking Him because He is Messiah, but rather because of the miracles He has done.

The boat arrives at the other side of the lake, where it seems that Jesus wants to rest from the journey they have been on and take some time to teach His disciples. As the text says,

John 6:3
3 But Jesus went up on the mountain, and there He sat with His disciples.

It's a wonderful moment in the story, as we see how Christ desires to spend time with His disciples, in spite of the persistent and expanding crowds. We are not sure which mountain He has taken them to; the word "mountain" here could simply refer to the hill country around the lake. But the mountain is not what's important. The idea is that Jesus wanted to be alone with those under His leadership.

John is setting the stage for the miracle. He has brought us up to speed on the "who," "what," and "where," and he is about to now reveal the "when." The text says,

John 6:4
4 Now the Passover, the feast of the Jews, was near.

The celebration of Passover is near. This is the second of three Passovers that John mentions (John 2:13, 6:4, and 13:1).

This would explain the large crowd following Jesus. They may have been gathering in preparation for the upcoming Passover Feast, and many would have made the pilgrimage there to Jerusalem together. But maybe there is another reason why John draws our attention to the fact that the Passover Feast was near. The Passover celebrated the death of the sacrificial lamb for the people, and in John 1:29, Jesus is said to be "the Lamb of God who takes away the sin of the world!" The Passover involved the eating of a lamb and of bread and this is one of the central ideas in this chapter.[2] Jesus even says later, in John 6:35, "I am the bread of life." So this becomes a great picture of God's provision for the people that is about to take place. There is a great parallel here.

But there is an issue on the horizon, which brings us to our first point: we see a problem among the crowd.

THE PROBLEM AMONG THE CROWD

The time of resting in Christ among the disciples has quickly come to a close. And John continues, saying,

John 6:5
5 So Jesus, after raising His eyes and seeing that a large crowd was coming to Him, said to Philip, "Where are we to buy bread so that these people may eat?"

The people had found Christ. They had most likely walked from miles away, and Jesus shows them great compassion, even though they were coming for the wrong reasons. All they wanted were signs and wonders, and Jesus presents them with grace.

Matthew and Luke tell us that not only did Jesus see them coming, but He ministered to their needs.

Matthew 14:14
14 When He came ashore, He saw a large crowd, and felt compassion for them and healed their sick.

Luke 9:11
11 He welcomed them and began speaking to them about the kingdom of God, and curing those who had need of healing.

---

[2] Grant Osborne, *John Verse by Verse* (Bellingham, WA: Lexham Press, 2018), 149.

Clearly, some time passes for which John's Gospel does not account. The details from Matthew and Luke reveal that the crowd had been there for a while, and that Jesus had ministered to them by healing and teaching. Luke 9:12 expands on this further.

Luke 9:12
12 Now the day was ending, and the twelve came up and said to Him, "Dismiss the crowd, so that they may go into the surrounding villages and countryside and find lodging and get something to eat; because here, we are in a secluded place."

And now Jesus, knowing the hearts of His disciples, begins a lesson. He presents a problem to the man who is from this area, someone who knows the landscape. (Also the man known for needing to see something to believe it.)

John 6:5
5 Therefore Jesus, lifting up His eyes and seeing that a large crowd was coming to Him, said to Philip, "Where are we to buy bread, so that these may eat?"

Jesus is saying, "We are not just going to send them away." In fact, in Luke 9:13 He says,

Luke 9:13
13 But He said to them, "You give them something to eat!" And they said, "We have no more than five loaves and two fish, unless perhaps we go and buy food for all these people."

The crowd presents two problems. On the surface, there isn't enough food to feed all of these people. But there is a much greater problem under the surface, a spiritual problem that Jesus knows is within His men. How does He know? Because Jesus is all-knowing.

John 6:6
6 This He was saying to test him, for He Himself knew what He was intending to do.

If we stop for just a moment here and get honest with ourselves we will have to admit that we have the same spiritual problem as the disciples.

You might be asking, what exactly *is* the problem? Let's look to Philip for our answer.

We can all relate to Philip. He calculates every situation in light of his own ability. He determines what's doable and what's not doable, based upon what he can do. But that's man's way. God doesn't work that way.

How many of us have problems that are much too large for us to handle, and yet the first thing we do is search for answers in our own strength? We think to ourselves, "How can I fix this problem?"

Remember what we said at the beginning of this chapter: men are like the gods they serve. The reality that I want you to see is that you and I live our lives by what we believe to be true about the God we worship. A weak view of God in your life will result in a weak life lived for God.

It seems like the disciples should have gotten it. These men lived with Jesus. They had seen water turned to wine. They had witnessed the official's son healed from afar. They saw Jesus heal a man who had been lame for thirty-eight years. You would expect their first thought to be, "Jesus can handle this problem." But what does Philip say?

John 6:7
7 Philip answered Him, "Two hundred denarii worth of bread is not enough for them, for each to receive just a little."

We can assume that maybe all they had at their disposal was two hundred denarii. What they had wasn't able to meet their need.

This reminded me of something that happened in my own life. I got a big doctor's bill right on the heels of a big tax bill, and my first response was, "I can't afford $8,000! Who walks around with $8,000?" An appropriate response would be more like, "Lord, You own the cattle on a thousand hills. You have met my needs. You have provided all I have needed in all of my forty-one years. I'm not going to forget Your ability. Lord, I'm going to rely on You. I remember Your provision for unexpected bills before, through a gracious brother in Christ. I remember when my kids were hungry, and I had nothing; by Your mercy, You worked in the heart of someone with resources, and You provided. How can I doubt for a moment that You will provide?"

Our faith can be so weak in the face of a crisis.

Notice how John points out that it's Jesus who sees the need.

John 6:5
5 So Jesus, after raising His eyes and seeing that a large crowd was coming to Him, said to Philip, "Where are we to buy bread so that these people may eat?"

It was Jesus who saw the need, not the disciples. And Jesus used this need to test them.

I wonder how many of us are simply being tested so that we can see how much faith we have? God will make a way! In spite of what it looks like, regardless of how helpless the situation seems, remember that God works all things together for good. He doesn't make all things good, because all things are not good, but rather,

Romans 8:28
28 And we know that God causes all things to work together for good to those who love God, to those who are called according to His purpose.

When we are facing the problems of life, as believers—"those who love God…those who are called according to His purpose"—we must remember that "God causes all things to work together for good." We must trust that He is able and learn to rely on the Lord first. Call upon Him. Seek His face.

But Philip reacts just like many of us would. Essentially, he says to Jesus, "We don't have enough money to take care of all these folks. Just send them home to eat somewhere else. Let someone else deal with their problem."

But Jesus has compassion. He has a plan, and His plan isn't dependent on others. God always has a way, and He will use that which is impossible for man to accomplish so that He is the only One who will receive the glory. We should always look for God to work in the "impossible."

The account continues to unfold as one of the other twelve disciples comes into the scene.

John 6:8–9
8 One of His disciples, Andrew, Simon Peter's brother, said to Him, 9 "There is a boy here who has five barley loaves and two fish; but what are these for so many people?"

This seems like an odd statement, but when you read the parallel account in Mark 6 it clarifies why Andrew told Jesus about the boy's lunch.

Mark 6:35–38
35 And when it was already late, His disciples came up to Him and said, "This place is secluded and it is already late; 36 send them away so that they may go into the surrounding countryside and villages and buy themselves something to eat." 37 But He answered them, "You give them something to eat!" And they said to Him, "Shall we go and spend two hundred denarii on bread and give it to them to eat?" 38 But He said to them, "How many loaves do you have? Go look!" And when they found out, they said, "Five, and two fish."

In other words, the disciples are saying, "We have only found a little food, but it isn't enough to feed 5,000 people." They have an impossible situation. It doesn't matter if it's 5,000 or 25,000 (which could have been the total number of people present), the reality is that we see the problem among the crowd. They don't have the resources they need to accomplish the task at hand. But even as we see the problem among the crowd, we can also see the solution among the crowd.

THE SOLUTION AMONG THE CROWD

John 6:10
10 Jesus said, "Have the people sit down." Now there was much grass in the place. So the men sat down, in number about five thousand.

Again, we know that there are a lot of people, and Mark gives us some detail about the instructions for how they were to sit. Can you imagine how difficult it would be to organize and seat a huge, hungry crowd? So what did Jesus, the Author of order, do?

Mark 6:39–40
39 And He commanded them all to sit down by groups on the green grass. 40 They sat down in groups of hundreds and of fifties.

They were placed in a manner that would allow order in the midst of the largest public miracle that has ever taken place.

John 6:10
10 Now there was much grass in the place. So the men sat down, in number about five thousand.

We know from Matthew's account that there were more, because it says,

Matthew 14:21
21 There were about five thousand men who ate, besides women and children.

There were 5,000 men, plus women and children—the problem was a very large problem. But the solution is right among the crowd, and the disciples are about to see something amazing. So Jesus instructs His men to go see how much food there is. As Matthew continues,

Matthew 14:17–18
17 They said to Him, "We have here only five loaves and two fish." 18 And He said, "Bring them here to Me."

Now we see what happens next. Keep in mind that this is the largest public miracle to ever take place. As we return to John, we read that,

John 6:11
11 Jesus then took the loaves, and having given thanks, He distributed to those who were seated; likewise also of the fish as much as they wanted.

Our Lord simply gives thanks, blesses the food, and gives it to all seated, as much bread and fish as they wanted.

If you have ever opened your eyes during a prayer of thanksgiving, this would be the time. Jesus is blessing the food. It's enough food for a child. The "loaves" are not like the loaves of bread we buy in the supermarket. They are like five small crackers, and they are accompanied by two small fish. And yet Christ simply gives thanks for the food and then "He distributed [both bread and fish] to those who were seated," and they ate until they were full. Matthew 14:20, Mark 6:42, and Luke 9:17 all say, "and they all ate and were satisfied."

Jesus was the solution to their problem, and He had been there the whole time. Christ had all the power necessary to take care of the problem, and He did it to teach them a lesson. The people could have gone home. They wouldn't have died if they weren't fed. But after a long day of teaching, healing, and miracles, Jesus wanted to make a final impact on all who were there, including His twelve disciples. He wanted to point them to the solution, to prove again that He was who He claimed to be.

It makes me wonder how much of what we go through in life is just to test us because we need to be reminded that Jesus is our solution.

Now John tells us what followed this major miracle,

John 6:12–13
12 When they were filled, He said to His disciples, "Gather up the leftover fragments so that nothing will be lost." 13 So they gathered them up, and filled twelve baskets with fragments from the five barley loaves which were left over by those who had eaten.

Notice the precision of Jesus' work. We are told that after the crowd had eaten, there was just enough left for the twelve disciples! They hadn't had their own meal because they had been busy serving.

There is a great lesson here for us. Serving takes sacrifice, and sacrifice isn't something people are willing to do for that which means little to them. When you serve the body, you are serving the Lord. But remember, we are like the gods we serve! Jesus served the people. Do you have a heart of service? It's important because Jesus has a heart of service, and so did His disciples.

We should be more like King David, who said, "I will not offer burnt offerings to the Lord my God which cost me nothing" (2 Sam 24:24).

These twelve disciples served the crowd self-sacrificially, and God provided perfectly for their needs as well. Sometimes we have to put off what we want so that others can get what they want or need. No doubt the disciples were hungry, but they were too busy serving the Lord by serving the people.

God blessed them with a small, personal basket of food for each man. Can you imagine providing for more than 5,000 people and having just the right and perfect amount left over for your workers? That's how God works. Now that we've seen the problem and the solution among the crowd, we'll look at the result among the crowd.

THE RESULT AMONG THE CROWD

The crowd wanted to make Him king. He could provide healing, He could raise the dead, He could outwit the religious leaders, and He could create a meal from nothing. What better candidate to be king? Thus John says,

John 6:14–15
14 Therefore when the people saw the sign which He had performed, they said, "This is truly the Prophet who is to come into the world." 15 So Jesus, perceiving that they were intending to come and take Him by force to make Him king, withdrew again to the mountain by Himself alone.

Jesus hadn't come to rule and reign as the earthly king that they wanted! He came to suffer and die, and these people couldn't grasp a Messiah who would serve and suffer. Make no mistake, He will come again, and He will reign as King when He comes! He will judge righteously when He comes, and those who seek after Him for what they can gain will be greatly disappointed.

They wanted Him to be their King, and He will, but not in the way that they desired. There is a great lesson here for us as we come to the end of this account. Whatever problems life brings us, God is able to overcome them. Christ is the solution, and it begins by trusting Him for salvation. He is and will always be Lord over our circumstances, and we can walk in that hope, trusting that God is able.

Proverbs 3:5–6
Trust in the LORD with all your heart And do not lean on your own understanding. In all your ways acknowledge Him, and He will make your paths straight.

When we place our trust in Him, God is with us and walks alongside us through life and the situations we will certainly face.

CHAPTER 2

CAUGHT IN A RAGING STORM
John 6:16–21

John 1:12
12 But as many as received Him, to them He gave the right to become children of God, even to those who believe in His name

The feeding of the 5,000 was an amazing event that gives us a greater understanding of who God is and how He does wondrous things. As numbers go, this is one of the greatest miracles we have seen—there were likely more than 25,000 people who Jesus fed with just a few loaves of bread.

And after organizing the people and feeding them until they were satisfied, Jesus had His disciples collect the leftovers, which came to just enough for twelve baskets; one for each man. The miracle was so astounding, that John 6:15 says that they wanted to take Jesus and make Him king.

John 6:15
15 So Jesus, perceiving that they were intending to come and take Him by force to make Him king, withdrew again to the mountain by Himself alone.

He knows it's not yet His time, so He withdrew again to the mountains, alone. Contextually, though, if we stop there, we miss a tremendous amount of helpful, even transformational, information.

As we approach John 6:16–21, there are four textual markers we need to look at. These four points will encourage us, and if we are willing to allow God to work, His Word will transform our lives.

Let's consider the following. First, the disciples got clear directions. Second, they made a critical decision. Third, they faced an intense danger. And finally, they experienced a miraculous deliverance!

Everyone who has purchased a copy of this book and is taking the time to read it has faced, or will face, storms in this life. The disciples, who at this moment are at a very high point in their journey with Jesus, are about to encounter a storm in their lives.

Problems and storms will always come. They will come when things are great and going as planned, and they will come when things aren't so great and not going as planned. They will come in good times and in bad times. The truth is that storms will appear on the horizon in just about every setting of life. Maybe there are raging storms in your life right now; maybe that's even the reason you are reading this book. Maybe no one knows about them or can see them. No one can hear the cries of the storms that are raging within your soul.

Let me remind you that when they come, how we deal with the storms that invade our lives will either mature and sanctify us more into the image of Christ or destroy us by controlling us, lying to us, and overtaking us. We will either grow up or give in. Either way, storms are coming. These men have no idea what is going to transpire in just a day's time. And while we don't need to walk around in fear of storms, we can all be encouraged to know that in the midst of the storms of life there is deliverance, there is hope, and there is a way out.

It may seem like there is no way to rid your life of the storms and struggles you face. It may seem impossible to escape the problems that are consuming you. But know that whatever you are facing, whether you're a believer or an unbeliever, there is a way you can find hope! With that in mind, let us consider our first point, that the disciples got clear directions.

CLEAR DIRECTIONS

Clearly, there are no directions here in our text. John begins in verse 16 with, "Now when evening came, His disciples went down to the sea." So you might be wondering why I would say that the disciples got clear directions.

Remember, however, that there are accounts from the other Gospels that can help fill in the gaps here in John. So why do I say that they got clear directions? We find the answer in Matthew 14 and Mark 6.

Remember, Jesus had just finished feeding the 5,000. Matthew's account goes like this, starting in verse 19,

Matthew 14:19–22
19 Ordering the people to sit down on the grass, He took the five loaves and the two fish, and looking up toward heaven, He blessed the food, and breaking the loaves He gave them to the disciples, and the disciples gave them to the crowds, 20 and they all ate and were satisfied. They picked up what was left over of the broken pieces, twelve full baskets. 21 There were about five thousand men who ate, besides women and children. 22 Immediately He made the disciples get into the boat and go ahead of Him to the other side, while He sent the crowds away.

After feeding the crowd, Matthew tells us that Jesus, "Immediately…made the disciples get into the boat and go ahead of Him to the other side." Why?

Recall that John 6:15 says that the people wanted to make Him king. Jesus didn't want His disciples to get entangled in this political agenda, so after feeding the people He gave them clear directions.

That said, it doesn't mean that today these directions are clear to us. Hundreds of years have passed, and things and places have changed over the centuries. So there is a bit of confusion about where Jesus had fed the crowd. Was it on the east side or the west side? There is also confusion as to exactly where it was that Jesus sent the disciples.

While Matthew states the fact of the directions, Mark is a bit more specific about where the men were directed to go.

Mark 6:45
Immediately Jesus made His disciples get into the boat and go ahead of Him to the other side to Bethsaida, while He Himself was sending the crowd away.

So now we know that they were given clear directions to head over to Bethsaida, but from where? Where was it that Jesus fed the 5,000? Was it on the east side, which seems to be more remote? Or was it on the west side, which seems to be more populated?

The obvious question is, where is Bethsaida? Because we know that they were instructed to "get into the boat and go ahead of Him to the other side to Bethsaida." So, if we can pinpoint Bethsaida, we should have a better idea as to where the feeding of the 5,000 took place.

There are actually two towns called Bethsaida—Bethsaida Julias and Bethsaida Galilee (I learned this from my trip to Israel)—but we can get to the main point from whichever side it took place. From my studies at this point, I think the feeding of the 5,000 took place on the northwest shore of Galilee. The historical site I visited is called Tabgha today. It is where you find the famous tile mosaic of the fish and basket on the floor of the church there, and the rock that tradition holds was the place where Jesus placed the bread to bless it. Who knows? I also had people try to sell me the stones that were used to slay Goliath.

Regardless, Jesus gives His disciples clear directions to go ahead of Him to Bethsaida, so they go. Next we will see that they made a critical decision.

A CRITICAL DECISION

The first thing we see is that they obeyed. They did what Jesus asked them to do, and they set sail to Bethsaida right away. And that brings us to where we pick up in John 6:16–17.

John 6:16–17
16 Now when evening came, His disciples went down to the sea, 17 and after getting into a boat, they started to cross the sea to Capernaum. It had already become dark, and Jesus had not yet come to them.

At first glance, we may think that this was the same trip to Bethsaida mentioned in Mark 6. Mark says that Jesus had instructed them to immediately go to Bethsaida, and when we come to John 6:16 it seems that they are simply obeying that instruction and going down to the boat. But I think this is the next day. Let me explain.

I believe that they have already made the trip across the sea to Bethsaida, and they have been waiting for Jesus. And Jesus doesn't show up when they expect Him to! The disciples are about to make a critical decision.

You see, sometimes the Lord gives us clear directions through His Word, and we obey and follow through. But isn't it true that, just like these men, it's easy to lose sight of what it was that the Lord has asked of us?

I believe the disciples became impatient. And because they went out on this unauthorized journey to Capernaum without Jesus, they got caught in the storm. I believe that many of the storms we face in life are because we haven't waited on God. We jump the gun. It's easy to do. As sinful humans, we can justify almost anything. Think about the following examples.

- God says, "Don't marry an unbeliever." But you think, "She's so pretty, and the timing seems perfect." Guard your heart!
- God gives you a calling to do something, and when you get there it's much harder than what you had imagined. The temptation is to give up and quit. Press on, friend, and don't grow weary in doing good.
- The Lord impresses on your heart to do something, but when you realize that it's going to take a lot longer than you expected, the temptation is to give in and change direction. Start that project for the glory of God. Do a little bit here and there, and over time you will accomplish much.

A mark of maturity in the Christian walk is endurance. It was Sinclair Ferguson who said, "The growing Christian keeps going…presses on, follows through, finishes well, doesn't give up…and at the end of the day…waits on God."[1]

Too many times, I believe we try to tell God what He is going to do. We try to make Him fit our plans, and we get frustrated when that doesn't happen. In this case, the disciples had a specific task, and that was to simply go to Bethsaida.

If you are tempted to give up on what you know the Lord has called you to do, remember what I heard H. B. Charles, Jr., say once, "The will of God is the safest place to be, but the safest place to be isn't always the will of God."

Just because we follow through with what God has called us to do doesn't mean there won't be storms. The disciples encountered storms when Jesus was with them and when He wasn't.

It really seems that they got impatient. Maybe they were thinking they might miss out on something. So, like the crowd, they went to search out Jesus. They didn't want to miss anything, so they set sail. Impatience is

---

[1] Sinclair B. Ferguson, *Maturity: Growing Up and Going On in the Christian Life.* (Edinburgh: Banner of Truth, 2019).

triggered when we have a goal, and we realize it's going to cost us more than we thought to reach it.

It's easy to imagine how they might have justified their decision—"Well, Jesus hasn't shown up. Maybe we didn't hear Him right. Maybe that instruction wasn't from above, but from dinner last night." We know, however, that we can be certain God's will never contradicts His Word.

What is it that God has asked of you that for a season, for a moment, you were good with, but something's changed? You were good for a time, but maybe you have become impatient and you are ready to take your boat to Capernaum. Like the disciples, you have a critical decision to make.

John 6:17
17 and after getting into a boat, they started to cross the sea to Capernaum. It had already become dark, and Jesus had not yet come to them.

They knew Jesus must be there. That is where everyone else went looking for Him.

John 6:24
24 So when the crowd saw that Jesus was not there, nor His disciples, they themselves got into the small boats, and came to Capernaum seeking Jesus.

So they set sail after dark. Most of the time, they would be out fishing at night, but that night wasn't the average night out on the water. That night, the decision to cast off and go somewhere that Jesus had not instructed them to go didn't play out well.

We have seen that the disciples got clear directions, we have seen that the disciples made a critical decision, and finally, we will see that the disciples faced an intense danger!

AN INTENSE DANGER

It had already become dark, and Jesus had not yet come to them. And now, as verse 18 says,

John 6:18
18 The sea began to be stirred up because a strong wind was blowing.

The Sea of Galilee lies about six hundred feet below sea level. Cool air from the southeast can rush in and displace the warm, moist air over the lake, churning up the water in a violent squall. In other words, a storm arose.

If you have never been in a boat in a storm, being tossed back and forth, then there is no way you can fully grasp these men's fear. I remember being on a fishing boat, headed back from Charleston, South Carolina, to fish a secret spot for a tournament. Out of the blue, a storm came up, and on that tossing boat in the middle of the rain and thunder and lighting, all I can remember is praying to the Lord to get us through the storm!

In the same way, out on the water in the midst of the storm, the disciples find themselves in the face of great danger. The storm is raging, and they are helpless. Remember that Jesus has gone off to the mountains to pray and seek time alone with the Father. In the midst of the crowds, Jesus understood His need to be alone. Maybe He wanted the disciples to take time that day to be alone.

Whatever the case, we are about to see more miracles take place. It's dark, and Jesus is up on a mountain overlooking the Sea of Galilee. Wherever He is, Mark 6:48 tells us that He could see them "straining at the oars."

Matthew 14:24
24 But the boat was already a long distance from the land, battered by the waves; for the wind was contrary.

They were in grave danger, and the boat was being tossed about and taking on water. In the Christian life, storms will come. They will come to the ones who honor the Lord and to the ones who dishonor the Lord.

James 1:4
4 And let endurance have its perfect result, so that you may be perfect and complete, lacking in nothing.

Romans 5:3
3 And not only this, but we also exult in our tribulations, knowing that tribulation brings about perseverance.

Storms will come. Some storms come from the decisions we make. Some storms come because of the Fall of man. And some storms come because the Lord allows them to grow us. The disciples fought to get out of this storm, but they were losing.

John 6:19
19 Then, when they had rowed about three or four miles

When I go to the gym looking for an extreme workout, I get on the rowing machine. But it's one thing to row a machine in the gym, and quite another to row an actual boat. And it's one thing to row a boat, and something very different to row a boat in a storm!

I can only imagine how worn out the disciples were. They probably had no fight left in them. And then, in the fourth watch of the night (between 3:00 and 6:00 a.m.), hope showed up.

We all will encounter danger in life, but with the Lord there is always hope. You may be facing danger today, but there is one who can overcome. The disciples got clear directions, made a critical decision, and faced an intense danger. And then they experienced a miraculous deliverance!

A MIRACULOUS DELIVERANCE

John 6:19
19 Then, when they had rowed about three or four miles, they saw Jesus walking on the sea and drawing near to the boat; and they were frightened.

This was not what they were expecting, and it scared them. In Matthew 14:26 we read,

Matthew 14:26
26 When the disciples saw Him walking on the sea, they were terrified, and said, "It is a ghost!" And they cried out in fear.

They were afraid of Him who came to help.

Maybe you're in the storms of life today. You're lost without Christ, and you're in great danger—not of simple, temporal death but of eternal separation from God. And now you are confronted with Jesus, the one who can save you, the one who can deliver you, the one who can calm the storms in your life. But you're afraid.

Maybe you're afraid of what your friends will think. Maybe you're afraid that your life will become boring. Maybe you're afraid that you will be rejected by your family or your culture. The enemy is telling you, "It's a great risk on your part."

The disciples were also afraid. But Jesus, miraculously walking on the water, leaves them no room for doubt.

Matthew 14:27
27 But immediately Jesus spoke to them, saying, "Take courage, it is I; do not be afraid."

Their deliverance showed up in the form of a miracle. Jesus is, once again, proving Himself to be God in flesh. He is showing Himself, once again, in complete authority over the creation. We all know that people can't walk on water. But Jesus isn't your average person. Therefore, fear not, for God is here.

Don't let fear hinder your willingness to receive Christ as your Savior. Yes, I lost friends. I miss out on things that I used to think were fun. I get mocked. But when Jesus bursts through the clouds, when I stand face-to-face with Him, there will be no greater joy than to be in His presence without fear. It is infinitely better to fear God than men.

Matthew 10:28
28 "Do not fear those who kill the body but are unable to kill the soul; but rather fear Him who is able to destroy both soul and body in hell."

Believe on the Lord Jesus Christ and receive, like the disciples, your deliverance. The text says,

John 6:21
21 So they were willing to receive Him into the boat, and immediately the boat was at the land to which they were going.

They sought to get to Capernaum on their own, but they couldn't make it. But when they were willing to receive Jesus into the boat, the text says that they made it to their destination immediately. It's a double miracle!

Are you willing to receive Jesus today? Because when you do, you are immediately saved. Who, today, will be saved? Who, today, will be encouraged to stay the course? Who, today, will be delivered from the storms of life by relying on Jesus?

CHAPTER 3

THE SUBSTANCE OF LIFE
John 6:16–21

Jesus Christ is the whole substance and only source of eternal life! You can't work your way to heaven. You can't earn your way. You can't buy your way. You can't even fly your way to heaven. The Bible is clear in Acts 4:12, that, "there is salvation in no one else; for there is no other name under heaven that has been given among men by which we must be saved." Jesus Himself says that He is the Bread of Life!

Just as Jesus offered the woman at the well living water (a drink by which she would never thirst again), here He identifies Himself as the Bread of Life. Jesus will offer Himself as the satisfying gift of God from above, the source of life, the substance of eternal life!

There are three main areas we will unpack in this passage, all of which we can relate to and be challenged by. First, we will look at the pursuit of the people; second, the problem of the people; and finally, the promise to the people.

THE PURSUIT

The crowd was in pursuit of Jesus. They had heard with their ears, some had seen with their eyes, and many had come from the feeding of the 5,000 that had taken place just a few days before. They are on the lookout for Jesus, the miracle-worker.

John 6:22
22 The next day the crowd that stood on the other side of the sea saw that there was no other small boat there, except one, and that Jesus had not entered with His disciples into the boat, but that His disciples had gone away alone.

It seems that we have the same group of people who were present at the feeding of the 5,000. It may be that they were looking for Him after He left the scene of the miracle, once again looking to make Him king. But they don't find Him. They only find an empty boat.

John 6:23–24

23 There came other small boats from Tiberias near to the place where they ate the bread after the Lord had given thanks. 24 So when the crowd saw that Jesus was not there, nor His disciples, they themselves got into the small boats, and came to Capernaum seeking Jesus.

After looking and not finding Jesus, they use small boats to get to Capernaum, where they think He might be. They are anxiously seeking Jesus. They are pursuing Him because of what He has done.

This portion of Scripture is a great place to pause, because it raises two questions that we all need to ask ourselves.

The first question is, are you even looking for Jesus in your life? Are we in pursuit of Him? Are we considering, or have we ever considered, the question of what kind of relationship we have with Jesus Christ? If we are not in pursuit of Jesus, then there is a problem.

Our relationship with Jesus isn't based upon a list of steps that must be completed. Our relationship with Jesus isn't simply about consistent ritual activities. Our relationship with Christ is about pursuing Him, spending time with Him, worshiping Him, and spending time with others talking about Him.

Maybe you think, "I just don't feel the need for Christ" (as if He is a commodity). And if you are really honest, you don't pursue Him. Not hourly, not daily, not weekly, not ever.

Your marriage is a wreck. Your kids are out of control. Your boss is ready to fire you. You have no drive. You don't seek the things of God, because you don't seek the Lord, and then you wonder, "Why is my life a mess?" It's a mess because, honestly, you care very little about Jesus Christ and His plans for your life. Instead, you spend much, if not most of the time very concerned about your plans rather than His. That's not a relationship. That's a divorce waiting to happen.

Just imagine if your marriage was like your relationship with Jesus Christ. Oh, that could never happen. Really?

John 6:66
66 As a result of this many of His disciples withdrew and were not walking with Him anymore.

After all of what we will look at in this passage, there will be a mass exodus of followers in chapter 6.

So the first question is, are you even looking for Jesus (pursuing Him) in your life? The second question is, if you are in pursuit of Jesus, are you pursuing Him for the right reason?

The crowd was not in pursuit of Jesus for the right reason. They sought after Him for what it would benefit them. But Jesus isn't a genie in a bottle. He paid for you, and if you are in Christ, you should be a slave to Christ. We should be in pursuit of Christ, but it must be for the right reasons—to glorify God through our lives and to point others to Jesus.

These people are in pursuit of Jesus, but they are pursuing Him for the wrong reason. How do we know?

John 6:25
25 When they found Him on the other side of the sea, they said to Him, "Rabbi, when did You get here?"

You and I would expect an answer to that question, but that isn't what He said, and this is where we come to our second point.

THE PROBLEM

They were looking for Jesus, and they found Him. Then they asked, "Rabbi, when did You get here?" John makes the point that Jesus did not address the immediate question but pursued the conversation at a much deeper level. He actually rebukes them.

John 6:26
26 Jesus answered them and said, "Truly, truly, I say to you, you seek Me, not because you saw signs, but because you ate of the loaves and were filled."

He is essentially saying, "You seek Me because I gave you food, and you're looking for food! You seek Me for what satisfies your personal desires. You do not seek Me because I'm God in flesh, or even because of the signs. You missed those. Rather, you seek Me for what you can gain."

No one likes to be used. If you are only interested in people for what you can get, you will soon be avoided. And if you only seek Christ for what He can do for you, then you will have problems like this crowd.

Jesus still knows the hearts of the people. They failed to recognize the signs, the miracles that pointed to the reality of who Jesus is. So, Jesus says,

John 6:27
27 "Do not work for the food which perishes, but for the food which endures to eternal life, which the Son of Man will give to you, for on Him the Father, God, has set His seal."

Jesus is our source of life, because the Father has made Him so. The people have a problem, and Jesus is pointing them to the solution, Himself. In the ancient world, a seal was a mark of ownership. Jesus knows that He is approved by God, so He speaks to them and they respond.

John 6:28–29
28 Therefore they said to Him, "What shall we do, so that we may work the works of God?" 29 Jesus answered and said to them, "This is the work of God, that you believe in Him whom He has sent."

The people have a problem. They want to know how they can do this work, so that they may work the works of God. They are simply saying, "We need to know how we can do some works to obtain salvation."

In Matthew 19:16, we see the same idea when the rich young ruler asked,

Matthew 19:16
16 "Teacher, what good thing shall I do that I may obtain eternal life?"

I love the point that Jesus makes here in John 6:29.

John 6:29
29 "This is the work of God, that you believe in Him whom He has sent."

He's saying, "You can't do anything. As a matter of fact, salvation is a work of God alone!" But that's not good enough for them. They've got more questions.

John 6:30–31
30 So they said to Him, "What then do You do for a sign, so that we may see, and believe You? What work do You perform? 31 Our fathers ate the manna in the wilderness; as it is written, 'HE GAVE THEM BREAD OUT OF HEAVEN TO EAT.'"

These people are truly blind to the truth. They are asking Jesus for a sign. They just ate food from heaven, and they need another sign. It's amazing how they bring in the Old Testament here, telling Jesus what God did. They really have no idea who He is.

John 6:32–33
32 Jesus then said to them, "Truly, truly, I say to you, it is not Moses who has given you the bread out of heaven, but it is My Father who gives you the true bread out of heaven. 33 For the bread of God is that which comes down out of heaven, and gives life to the world."

He is saying, "God, not Moses, gave your fathers bread." They simply can't see. They are not enlightened by the Holy Spirit. The crowd's problem is that they don't believe; they are false followers. No sign will save them. Only a touch from above can open anyone's eyes. Jesus patiently deals with their problems.

John 6:34
34 Then they said to Him, "Lord, always give us this bread."

In other words, "Feed us. Give us what we want." They have completely missed what Jesus said in verses 32 and 33, that He is the bread. So He clarifies,

John 6:35–36
35 Jesus said to them, "I am the bread of life; he who comes to Me will not hunger, and he who believes in Me will never thirst. 36 But I said to you that you have seen Me, and yet do not believe."

I'm reminded here of Hebrews 4:2, where it says,

Hebrews 4:2
2 For indeed we have had good news preached to us, just as they also; but the word they heard did not profit them, because it was not united by faith in those who heard.

Jesus is speaking to the people, but they aren't hearing. They have a problem that I would call the "me" syndrome. But Jesus is here, and He has come for one purpose alone: to do the will of the Father.

John 6:37–40
37 All that the Father gives Me will come to Me, and the one who comes to Me I will certainly not cast out. 38 For I have come down from heaven, not to do My own will, but the will of Him who sent Me. 39 This is the will of Him who sent Me, that of all that He has given Me I lose nothing, but raise it up on the last day. 40 For this is the will of My Father, that everyone who beholds the Son and believes in Him will have eternal life, and I Myself will raise him up on the last day."

The people's problem is that they don't believe. They are looking for something that will equal belief, but it isn't coming. Jesus is on-task to save the elect, and the elect are the "whosoever wills." His desire is to save them and raise them!

John 6:40
40 "For this is the will of My Father, that everyone who beholds the Son and believes in Him will have eternal life, and I Myself will raise him up on the last day."

What you believe about Jesus Christ is important! The question is, have you placed your faith (your belief) in Jesus Christ, and have you beheld the Son of God as Lord of your life? And do you believe that in Him alone you can be saved? If not, then today is the day to place your faith in Him, because that was His purpose for coming. Those standing around, hearing all that is happening, have become frustrated. Now the Jews are ready to jump in.

John 6:41–42
41 Therefore the Jews were grumbling about Him, because He said, "I am the bread that came down out of heaven." 42 They were saying, "Is this not Jesus, the son of Joseph, whose father and mother we know? How does He now say, 'I have come down out of heaven'?"

From a human perspective, these are legitimate questions. But the people have a problem. They don't see Jesus for who He is. They miss the fact of the virgin birth (the conception of Jesus Christ from above). They miss the fact that He is the fulfillment of prophecy, and they ask a rhetorical question. They are basically calling Him a liar, but Jesus is about to stop it.

John 6:43
43 Jesus answered and said to them, "Do not grumble among yourselves."

He is simply stating, "Don't try, in your limited minds, to arrange all this in your heads, because it's not going to happen. And I'll tell you why." What comes next is big.

John 6:44
44 "No one can come to Me unless the Father who sent Me draws him; and I will raise him up on the last day."

He is saying, "You can't understand unless the Father gives you that ability, but the ones that He draws will come." Do you feel that drawing, to come to Jesus and be saved, to change your life by trusting in Him for salvation and/or sanctification? Don't turn away from that drawing. It is from God, and those He draws, He will raise.

John 6:45–47
45 "It is written in the prophets, 'AND THEY SHALL ALL BE TAUGHT OF GOD.' Everyone who has heard and learned from the Father, comes to Me. 46 Not that anyone has seen the Father, except the One who is from God; He has seen the Father. 47 Truly, truly, I say to you, he who believes has eternal life."

Will you believe? Jesus is the source of life, and it takes a total commitment—a complete, absolute surrender to Christ. If you are being drawn by God unto salvation, place your faith in Jesus now, because He says,

John 6:48–50
48 "I am the bread of life. 49 Your fathers ate the manna in the wilderness, and they died. 50 This is the bread which comes down out of heaven, so that one may eat of it and not die."

Jesus says, "I'm the source of life."

John 6:51

51 "I am the living bread that came down out of heaven; if anyone eats of this bread, he will live forever; and the bread also which I will give for the life of the world is My flesh."

What? That statement got the Jews' attention.

John 6:52

52 Then the Jews began to argue with one another, saying, "How can this man give us His flesh to eat?"

They have a problem, yet again. They are completely missing what Jesus is saying.

THE PROMISE

The Jews are outraged by this statement. And the idea of Jesus literally giving His flesh to be eaten is outrageous. But they missed what Jesus was really saying. He was not referring to what is called transubstantiation, meaning the Lord's table literally becomes the blood and body of Jesus.

Throughout the Scriptures, the idea of Jesus giving Himself sacrificially for sinners is repeated over and over. All Jesus is saying here is, "I am your source of life. I am your substance for life." And His promise to the people is one that will shatter them.

John 6:53–56

53 So Jesus said to them, "Truly, truly, I say to you, unless you eat the flesh of the Son of Man and drink His blood, you have no life in yourselves. 54 He who eats My flesh and drinks My blood has eternal life, and I will raise him up on the last day. 55 For My flesh is true food, and My blood is true drink. 56 He who eats My flesh and drinks My blood abides in Me, and I in him."

The Jews were not to eat food with any blood, and to their ears this sounds like cannibalism. It seemed so outrageous that it was beyond their ability to process.

Jesus, of course, was not speaking of literally eating His flesh and drinking His blood. These are metaphors that refer to the necessity of accepting Jesus' death on the cross as the only source of eternal life.

Jesus meant that there must be a deep partaking of Him. We must live as if He is truly the source of life. We must take the promise of God here to mean that we must fully partake of Christ!

You can take and hold bread. You can eat that bread, and it's filling. Is Jesus as real to you as bread? Take and believe, because "unless you eat the flesh of the Son of Man and drink His blood, you have no life in yourselves." Unless you take hold of Jesus Christ and believe in Him, you will die and be eternally separated from Him. He promises life. He is the source of life. He is the Bread of Life of which you must take and eat.

John 6:57–58
57 "As the living Father sent Me, and I live because of the Father, so he who eats Me, he also will live because of Me. 58 This is the bread which came down out of heaven; not as the fathers ate and died; he who eats this bread will live forever."

Will you partake? Will you believe, and be saved, and live?

John 6:59–60
59 These things He said in the synagogue as He taught in Capernaum. 60 Therefore many of His disciples, when they heard this said, "This is a difficult statement; who can listen to it?"

You may be saying the same things, but you have a choice to believe or to reject that Jesus is Lord.

CHAPTER 4

THE DESERTION OF THE DISCIPLES
John 6:61–71

As we begin studying this portion of the Word, it's helpful to understand the main idea of the passage. The thrust of this text deals with those who are claiming to be followers of Christ, but in the end are actually deserters of Christ. The definition of "desert" is "to withdraw from or leave, usually without intent to return"[1] That's exactly how this passage describes the actions of those who will walk away from the faith!

If you have been investing your time, talents, and treasure in people, you know that not everyone you put effort into will continue walking with Christ. Therefore, we must assume that not everyone who professes Jesus Christ is truly born again! Because if that were the case, then eternal security would be based upon some kind of human effort or merit.

Just as Matthew recorded in his gospel,

Matthew 7:21
21 "Not everyone who says to Me, 'Lord, Lord,' will enter the kingdom of heaven, but he who does the will of My Father who is in heaven will enter."

The proof of your salvation—the verification, the confirmation, the evidence that you are truly born from above—is that you continue walking with Him, because when you are born again you will always be a child of God. If your children go off the deep end, are they still your children? Of course! They still have your DNA. They will continue to look like you in many ways as long as they live! Once you conceive a child, that child will always be your child because he or she is born of you. But what if you're adopted? Adopted children have equal rights, just like biological children. You're a child of your parents just like the other children. Maybe you don't have the same DNA, but you're an heir and rightful member of that family. That's what happens when you are adopted into a family.

---

[1] *Merriam Webster Online*, s.v. "Desert, *n.*," accessed March 24, 2023, https://www.merriam-webster.com/dictionary/desert

Being a Christian is much the same. When you are born from above, it is a lasting, irrevocable, sustaining, secure salvation, because you are a child of God—not by any means on your own, but rather of God (Titus 3:4–5). And as a child of God, you are an heir of God. And an heir has rights.

John 10:28–29
28 "and I give eternal life to them, and they will never perish; and no one will snatch them out of my hand. 29 My Father, who has given them to Me, is greater than all; and no one is able to snatch them out of the Father's hand."

As Christians, we are secure in Christ if we are indeed born again of Christ. However, we need to make sure we understand that not everyone who says that he or she is a follower of Jesus is truly born again. Some follow Jesus like seagulls follow a shrimp boat. They aren't following the boat; rather, they are following the bait, the resources that the boat offers. Like the birds, they want what they can get from Jesus, so they follow Him with wrong motives.

When we're truly born from above, we are sealed by the Holy Spirit. He confirms our status in God's family. Thus we read,

Ephesians 4:30
30 Do not grieve the Holy Spirit of God, by whom you were sealed for the day of redemption.

I am convinced that those who have placed their sole trust in Christ unto salvation are absolutely secure. Paul says it this way in Romans 8,

Romans 8:38–39
38 For I am convinced that neither death, nor life, nor angels, nor principalities, nor things present, nor things to come, nor powers, 39 nor height, nor depth, nor any other created thing, will be able to separate us from the love of God that is in Christ Jesus our Lord.

Once we are saved by the almighty God, we're saved and we will continue walking with Him. This is what we call the perseverance of the saints. It describes those in whom He began a work, and He will see it to completion.

Notice that I didn't say that we would be perfect, but rather, we will not walk away from the faith, reject Christ, and reject the Holy Spirit. If we do walk away (and reject Christ and the Holy Spirit), then we were never saved in the first place. Why can I say that? We find the answer in 2 Corinthians 5.

2 Corinthians 5:17
17 Therefore if anyone is in Christ, he is a new creature; the old things passed away; behold, new things have come.

And from our text earlier, John 6:51, we are reminded,

John 6:51
51 "I am the living bread that came down out of heaven; if anyone eats of this bread, he will live forever; and the bread also which I will give for the life of the world is My flesh."

Over and over, we are told that eternal life is secure, because it's based upon the words and works of Jesus Christ. And so we have to recognize that not everyone who claims to be a Christian is born from above.

What we find in our current passage is a contrast of persons. We find a side-by-side contrast of false versus true followers of Christ. We see this in the contrast of the desertion of the disciples (John 6:60–66) and the dependence of the disciples (John 6:67–71).

There are two main points that I want us to consider as we come to this section of God's Word. First, we will look at the characteristics of a false disciple. And then, in contrast, we will consider the characteristics of a true disciple.

THE CHARACTERISTICS OF A FALSE DISCIPLE

In the last chapter we studied Jesus' statements that He is the Bread of Life. The Jews are outraged that Jesus made that claim.

John 6:54–56
54 "He who eats My flesh and drinks My blood has eternal life, and I will raise him up on the last day. 55 For My flesh is true food, and My blood is true drink. 56 He who eats My flesh and drinks My blood abides in Me, and I in him."

And not only does this stir up the Jews, but many of Jesus' "disciples" begin to express doubt.

John 6:60
60 Therefore many of His disciples, when they heard this said, "This is a difficult statement; who can listen to it?"

The passage continues by characterizing these false disciples. John starts out by pointing out that they are marked by grumbling.

John 6:61
61 But Jesus, conscious that His disciples grumbled at this, said to them, "Does this cause you to stumble?"

This is exactly what the Jews were doing previously, as we find in verse 41.

John 6:41
41 Therefore the Jews were grumbling about Him, because He said, "I am the bread that came down out of heaven."

They didn't believe Him, and all they could do was grumble about the truth. What we find here is the very same thing. Jesus is speaking, and what He speaks is truth. These "disciples" have a hard time hearing the truth, so they grumble about it.

The Greek word (μαθητής) which translates as "disciple" here simply means, "one who engages in learning through instruction from another, pupil, apprentice."[2]

These were His students. They were following and learning, but like many students who get hit with the meat of the Word, they didn't like the truth and they grumbled. These men were marked by complaining about what Jesus was teaching. Essentially they're saying, "We are good with You feeding us and giving us what we want, but don't tell us anything we don't want to hear." They are acting just like the grumbling Jews of verse 41.

---

[2] William Arndt, Frederick William Danker, and Walter Bauer, *A Greek-English Lexicon of the New Testament and Other Early Christian literature*, 3rd ed. (Chicago: University of Chicago Press, 2000), 609.

Jesus only ever speaks truth, and the text says that His disciples grumbled at this. The Greek word here for "grumble" means, "to be offended or to express oneself in low tones of disapprobation, grumble, murmur."[3]

I believe that our culture is marked by false disciples. We live among a plurality of "disciples." So many churches and pastors are simply scared to be honest with the Word of God. They are embarrassed by what they believe to be true from God's Holy Word, so they make ways around it.

Do you know people who claim to be disciples of Christ, yet grumble at His truth? They don't like the truth about a certain topic, so they twist it or use a bad hermeneutic to do away with the issue, or they simply avoid talking about those topics.

For example, take the issue of homosexuality. It's a sin. You can't be of Christ and live in sin knowingly without conviction and desire to change. Yet the false disciples will claim that homosexuals are simply born that way. The problem is we were all born with a sin nature, but we can't do everything we feel like doing because we were "born" to behave that way.

Psalm 51 warns us that we are all equally are born into sin. My sin may not be your sin, but we can all be certain that we are born into sin and separation from God.

Psalm 51:5
Behold, I was brought forth in iniquity,
And in sin my mother conceived me.

Let's take the role of women in ministry as another example. There are biblical roles for both women and men. God calls women to do certain things and He calls men to do certain things. But this, again, isn't popular.

Our culture has made young men timid to the point that they won't express that what the Bible says is true about the roles of men and women, lest they be called a male chauvinist. Be encouraged to never be fearful to call what God calls good, good! Rather, woe to us who call evil things "good," and good things "evil."

---

[3] Arndt, Danker, and Bauer, *A Greek-English Lexicon*, 204.

The topic of abortion provides a final example. Murder is murder, and life begins at conception. But false disciples grumble and complain. They take offense or they give up believing. This is because, in their eyes, what they believe to be true is more true than what Jesus says is true. That makes them their own final authority, their own "god." And that is idolatry.

A characteristic of a false disciple is one who grumbles about God's truth rather than embracing it. In verse 61, Jesus asks them, "Does this cause you to stumble?" He follows this question with another in verse 62.

John 6:62
62 "What then if you see the Son of Man ascending to where He was before?"

Jesus is saying, "Would you believe me then? You look for signs, for proof so that you will believe and can be confident in your salvation." He knows that even if He returned to the Father right before their eyes they still wouldn't believe.

John 1:1–5
1 In the beginning was the Word, and the Word was with God, and the Word was God. 2 He was in the beginning with God. 3 All things came into being through Him, and apart from Him nothing came into being that has come into being. 4 In Him was life, and the life was the Light of men. 5 The Light shines in the darkness, and the darkness did not comprehend it.

Their hearts were hard. In Luke 16:31, we are reminded that,

Luke 16:31
"If they do not listen to Moses and the Prophets, they will not be persuaded even if someone rises from the dead."

After His rhetorical question in John 6:62, Jesus transitions in verse 63, saying,

John 6:63
63 "It is the Spirit who gives life; the flesh profits nothing; the words that I have spoken to you are spirit and are life."

He is simply saying, "You have a hard time with the idea of eating of My flesh. Partake of the Spirit. It's the Spirit that imparts life. My Word, the very words which I speak and have spoken to you, are Spirit and life."

Salvation comes by hearing the Word of God. "In the beginning was the Word" (John 1:1). It's the Spirit who gives life. And if the words of Jesus are Spirit, then the very Word which He speaks is life-giving.

Don't grumble about Gods' Word, because it's the very thing that imparts life. Embrace God's truth. Hold fast to God's truth. Be unashamed of God's truth. If we grumble or take offense or we give up believing, what do we have to stand on? The one who gives life was speaking truth to them, and they wanted nothing to do with Him or His teachings.

The first characteristic of a false disciple is grumbling about the life-giving words of Jesus. If you want to help someone, don't pat them on the back while they are going to hell! Tell them that you love them. Show them that you love them. But do this while gently giving them the life-giving words of Jesus.

Maybe you have grumbled and complained about the message of salvation. You have taken offense, thinking, "How dare you claim that Jesus is the only way someone can get to heaven?" Know that it's His Word that says He is the only way. Don't reject the life-giving words of Jesus! Don't become bitter because there are things that you don't like or have been sold by the culture. Don't be like the false disciples.

The first characteristic of a false disciple is grumbling. The second is not believing.

Again we find John using parallels between the disciples and the Jews. The Jews in verse 41 grumbled. Notice that they also failed to believe.

John 6:42–44
42 They were saying, "Is not this Jesus, the son of Joseph, whose father and mother we know? How does He now say, 'I have come down out of heaven'?" 43 Jesus answered and said to them, "Do not grumble among yourselves. 44 No one can come to Me unless the Father who sent Me draws him."

They are lost Jews living in unbelief. You can't follow Jesus and live in unbelief. You can't claim to be a disciple of Christ and not believe in Him.

John 6:63–64
63 "It is the Spirit who gives life; the flesh profits nothing; the words that I have spoken to you are spirit and are life. 64 But there are some of you who do not believe."

Jesus is saying, "I am the way, the truth, and the life, but some of you don't believe." Jesus knows this because He is all-knowing. He is deity. He walks on water, He raises the dead, He gives spiritual life, He forgives sin, He heals the sick. And He is all-knowing. And as He continues speaking, He says,

John 6:64
64 "But there are some of you who do not believe." For Jesus knew from the beginning who they were who did not believe, and who it was that would betray Him.

It is interesting to think that Jesus, knowing all who would desert Him, is teaching them the very thing that would reveal their unbelief.

You can fake being His follower. You can fool your own family about your hidden unbelief about Jesus. You can memorize all the right verses, and you can say all the right things. You can echo what you hear from those who surround you. But in the end, you can't hide your heart from Jesus.

My heart breaks for pretenders and false disciples. The only ones they hurt are themselves.

Our culture is at a place where unbelieving "Christians" have been coming out of the closet in greater and greater numbers. You may even know someone who has said something to the effect of, "Mom and Dad, I know you love Jesus, but I don't want anything to do with your Jesus anymore. I don't want to be part of your religion."

If that's you, so be it. Stop faking it. Come out of the closet, and stop trying to be something you're not, because your unbelief marks how lost you are. It all ends the same way it ends here in our text.

You might be thinking this is a harsh approach, but would you rather your child hide this from you or be honest with you? I would rather embrace an unbelieving child than have an unbelieving child who is pretending to be a believer and is headed to hell!

If it was my own child, he or she is still going to church and sitting under the preaching of God's Word. And God's Word will do one of two things: it will change your heart, or it will be so offensive to you that it will drive you to be honest with yourself and others.

We have to remember that no matter how much we want our own children to be born from above, it is entirely a work of God.

John 6:65
65 And He was saying, "For this reason I have said to you, that no one can come to Me unless it has been granted him from the Father."

My prayer is for a mighty work, and when there is grumbling and unbelief in the heart of man, it takes a work of God.

We've seen that grumbling about the Word of God and unbelief in the heart are characteristics of a false disciple. But there is one more characteristic of a false disciple revealed in our passage—rejection of the truth. The life-giving, Spirit-filled, Word of Jesus was rejected because it was offensive and convicting. Because of their lack of faith and their unbelief, the text says,

John 6:66
66 As a result of this many of His disciples withdrew and were not walking with Him anymore.

Here have the disciples' complete desertion of Christ. This group of followers who had come so close to the Messiah has departed from Him. John MacArthur writes in his commentary on the book of John that they had "abandoned any further pretense of being His followers, they deserted Him and joined the scoffers who had rejected Jesus outright."[4] They walked away from the only One who could give them life.

---

[4] John MacArthur, *John 1–11*, MacArthur New Testament Commentary, Vol. 11 (Chicago: Moody Publishers, 2006), 266.

Notice that this falling away was a progression. It didn't happen in just one moment. It was a process.

This is a good point to examine our own hearts. Are you offended by the truth of God's Word? Do you have unbelief in your heart? As we have seen, those things will lead you to desert the truth, to walk away from all we know to be true about Jesus, the gospel, and salvation. If these characteristics describe you, I pray that God will change your heart and reveal Himself to you in a way that only He can do, through the working of the Holy Spirit in your life.

Now that we've looked at the characteristics of a false disciple, let's consider the characteristics of a true disciple.

THE CHARACTERISTICS OF A TRUE DISCIPLE

From verse 66, we are not sure just how many departed, but there was a mass exodus.

John 6:67
67 So Jesus said to the twelve, "You do not want to go away also, do you?"

Jesus is asking the twelve disciples, "Do you, like them, want to desert Me?" It's a question that I think is relevant, but odd, because He already knew the answer, as we saw in verse 64.

John 6:64
64 "But some of you do not believe." For Jesus knew from the beginning who they were who did not believe, and who it was that would betray Him.

Peter answers Jesus in John 6:68.

John 6:68
68 Simon Peter answered Him, "Lord, to whom shall we go? You have words of eternal life."

The first characteristic of a true disciple is that he (or she) knows where he should be. Peter answers Jesus with a rhetorical question of his own, "Lord, to whom shall we go?" He is essentially saying, "We know where we are to be, even if we did not understand when you told us to 'eat My flesh and drink My blood.'"

There were many teachers they could have followed, but there were none like Jesus. The twelve have seen with their eyes and heard with their ears, and while they are far from perfect men, they are faithful.

Peter, the spokesmen for the group, speaks a word of confession, allegiance, and belief. Interestingly, these words are in stark contrast to the false disciples who abandoned Jesus. They don't even know where they are going, but they will be faithful to continue to follow even as many others are walking away.

Don't be surprised in life if you see people walk away from the faith. Let them follow whatever it is they are following, but don't you lose sight of Jesus. Peter points to the reality that he and the other disciples know, that Jesus has the "words of eternal life."

A second characteristic of a true disciple is belief, just the opposite of a false disciple.

Peter continues in verse 69,

John 6:69
69 "We have believed and have come to know that You are the Holy One of God."

The Scripture is very clear that one must believe in the Lord Jesus Christ to be saved. These men left their jobs and followed Jesus. Faith and belief are characteristics of a true disciple, and they should always result in action. And through that faith, belief, and action you will come to know God in a mighty way, just as these men came to know that Jesus is the Holy One of God.

Jesus isn't done yet, because He knows all things. He knows there is still one in hiding, that there is a false disciple among them who hasn't yet walked away.

We are warned that the church will have tares (false disciples) mixed with the wheat (true disciples). Know the truth and be aware, because dangerous false disciples may walk among us like wolves in sheep's clothing.

John 6:70
70 Jesus answered them, "Did I Myself not choose you, the twelve, and yet one of you is a devil?"

Regarding the one referred to as "a devil," I believe Jesus is talking about position (chosen for a role) not about salvation (chosen for election). Later, when the devil leaves the upper room, Jesus talks about that choosing in John 15:16.

John 15:16
16 "You did not choose Me but I chose you, and appointed you that you would go and bear fruit, and that your fruit would remain, so that whatever you ask of the Father in My name He may give to you."

We know to whom Jesus is referring as a devil. He wasn't surprised, and John didn't leave that as a surprise to us, as he writes in verse 71,

John 6:71
71 Now He meant Judas the son of Simon Iscariot, for he, one of the twelve, was going to betray Him.

I find that Christ knowing this points to His supernatural patience. He continued His ministry all the way to the cross knowing that Judas was going to betray Him, like the others who had just walked away. He still showers the man with grace, love, and compassion. He didn't kick Judas out; He let him make that choice.

How about you? Will you desert Jesus or believe in Him?

CHAPTER 5

TIMING IS EVERYTHING
John 7:1–13

Timing is everything. That is such a true statement! The older I get and the longer I walk with the Lord in this Christian life, I have come to see, understand, and believe that timing is everything.

God is a timely God. In John 7:8 we read Jesus' words about timing.

John 7:8
8 "Go up to the feast yourselves; I do not go up to this feast because My time has not yet fully come."

In John 2, we saw Jesus speak about timing in verse 4.

John 2:4
4 And Jesus said to her, "Woman, what does that have to do with us? My hour has not yet come."

In John 8, we will see Jesus speak about timing in verse 20.

John 8:20
20 These words He spoke in the treasury, as He taught in the temple; and no one seized Him, because His hour had not yet come.

We see yet another example of timing addressed in John 13:1.

John 13:1
1 Now before the Feast of the Passover, Jesus, knowing that His hour had come that He would depart out of this world to the Father, having loved His own who were in the world, He loved them to the end.

And another example in John 17:1.

John 17:1
1 Jesus spoke these things; and lifting up His eyes to heaven, He said, "Father, the hour has come; glorify Your Son, that the Son may glorify You."

There was a certain time frame for Jesus, but that is not the only time frame addressed in God's Word. There is a time for grace, as we see in Psalm 102:13.

Psalm 102:13
13 You will arise and have compassion on Zion; For it is time to be gracious to her, For the appointed time has come.

There is an eschatological time frame, as we see in Acts 1:7.

Acts 1:7
7 He said to them, "It is not for you to know times or epochs which the Father has fixed by His own authority."

In Ecclesiastes 3:1–8, we are reminded of these truths about time.

Ecclesiastes 3:1–8
1 There is an appointed time for everything. And there is a time for every event under heaven--2 A time to give birth and a time to die; A time to plant and a time to uproot what is planted. 3 A time to kill and a time to heal; A time to tear down and a time to build up. 4 A time to weep and a time to laugh; A time to mourn and a time to dance. 5 A time to throw stones and a time to gather stones; A time to embrace and a time to shun embracing. 6 A time to search and a time to give up as lost; A time to keep and a time to throw away. 7 A time to tear apart and a time to sew together; A time to be silent and a time to speak. 8 A time to love and a time to hate; A time for war and a time for peace.

You see, timing is everything. There was and is a divine timetable off of which God works. Simply stated, God is in absolute control. Do you know that God is sovereign? He hasn't lost His grip on you or on your circumstances, and that is easier to see when we understand that timing is everything.

So let's begin by looking at where we have been, where we are, where we are going, and how this portion of Scripture emphasizes the importance of God's timing, even for our own lives today.

If you recall from chapter 6, Jesus was ministering to the needs of the people He met on the Sea of Galilee. Jesus has performed amazing miracles, feeding some 25,000 people with just a few loaves of bread and walking on water. He then delivers the "Bread of Life" discourse, resulting in a falling away of false disciples.

These false followers couldn't handle the truth, and in John 6:66 we learn,

John 6:66
66 As a result of this many of His disciples withdrew and were not walking with Him anymore.

The reality is that many followers simply walked away. They were OK with the miraculous food and healing (both of which drew huge crowds). But when it came to the truth, they withdrew and were not walking with Him any longer.

From this point forward, public hostility against Jesus begins to grow. This is also the point at which His ministry shifts from public to private. In the private ministry of Jesus, He focuses His attention on the twelve disciples.

In light of understanding that timing is everything in the portion of Scripture we're beginning to look at, there are four things to consider and understand. First, we will examine the reason. Second, we will consider the request. Third, we will unpack the response. And finally, we will look at the reaction.

THE REASON

Chapter 7 of John begins by saying,

John 7:1
1 After these things Jesus was walking in Galilee, for He was unwilling to walk in Judea because the Jews were seeking to kill Him.

John starts out by saying, "After these things." This transition from chapter 6 to chapter 7 isn't perfectly clear chronologically. "After these things" took place, five or six months had passed. (We will unpack this chronology when we get to verse 2.)

Jesus is walking and working in Galilee. The reality is that He was unwilling at this time to walk and work in Judea (Jerusalem).

Why?

John 7:1
1 After these things Jesus was walking in Galilee, for He was unwilling to walk in Judea because the Jews were seeking to kill Him.

This is a big deal to the non-Jew. Early in the Gospel of John, we are reminded that,

John 1:11
11 He came to His own, and those who were His own did not receive Him.

And because of that, He went out from them and began to share the message of salvation to all the world, both to Jews and Gentiles. So Jesus is there in Galilee preaching, teaching, and doing miraculous signs and wonders. But there is a storm brewing. He has made people angry. Although this is nothing new; it is something that has escalated, and it is now a burning desire in the hearts of the religious leaders.

We need to note that Jesus isn't trying to keep away from persecution. But because He knows all things, He knows that if He goes where these religious leaders are, they will have His neck.

We can learn a great lesson from this. There is a time to die, and there is a time to live, and Jesus, the King, is on this divine time schedule. Here, He simply postpones His death.

I think that we, as Christians, sometimes are unwise and presume on the grace of God when we knowingly walk into a hostile situation to preach the gospel of Christ. Of course there is a time for that, but the prompting of Spirit of God must be clear.

Jesus was perfectly in tune with the Father's will. And it wasn't yet His time. Remember that timing is everything, and Jesus isn't willing to give up His life at this time. Notice that I say, "give," because no one can take it from Him. He was willing to give up His life for yours and mine.

John 10:18
18 "No one has taken it away from Me, but I lay it down on My own initiative. I have authority to lay it down, and I have authority to take it up again. This commandment I received from My Father."

He is in absolute control. God is working in the perfect timing of His absolute sovereignty. It was perfect timing when Christ was born.

Galatians 4:4
4 But when the time had fully come, God sent His Son, born of a woman, born under the Law.

It was perfect timing when Christ died, as well.

John 12:23
23 And Jesus answered them, saying, "The hour has come for the Son of Man to be glorified."

But here, in the context of our passage, it wasn't the right time. And the religious leaders had already begun plotting to kill Jesus in John 5:18.

John 5:18
18 For this reason therefore the Jews were seeking all the more to kill Him, because He not only was breaking the Sabbath, but also was calling God His own Father, making Himself equal with God.

So we understand the reason why, in John 7:1, Jesus "was unwilling to walk in Judea." It was simply not His time to die. The text continues,

John 7:2
2 Now the feast of the Jews, the Feast of Booths, was near.

This is how we know five or six months has lapsed between chapter 6 and chapter 7. If you recall, when Jesus fed the 5,000, the time of the Passover was near (John 6:4). Here we are at the time of the Feast of the Booths. This is a harvest feast, one of three festivals that required the attendance of every Jewish male. It was a feast that celebrated God's provision in wilderness, so they would build booths with roofs made from branches, and camp out in them as a reminder of how God provided for their needs.

"It was a daily ritual that took place! The people would, each morning, gather at the temple and they would come with an etrog (citrus fruit) in their left hand, and a lulab in their right hand. This was a combination of three different branches (palms, willow, and myrtle), and once everyone was ready and gathered, the priest would hold out a golden pitcher and head towards the pool of Siloam. The people would wave their lulabs in rhythm and sing different psalms, and when they approached the pool of Siloam, the priest would dip the golden pitcher and gather water, while the people would recite some beautiful words from Isaiah 12:3. The crowds would march back to the temple, going through the Water Gate with trumpets blasting. They would circle the altar and pour out the water. This was a daily event." [1]

This was what was happening during the Feast of the Booths, and Jesus seems unwilling to go. But He has good reason. At this point Jesus' brothers appear, and they made a request of Him.

THE REQUEST

John 7:3–5
3 Therefore His brothers said to Him, "Leave here and go into Judea, so that Your disciples also may see Your works which You are doing. 4 For no one does anything in secret when he himself seeks to be known publicly. If You do these things, show Yourself to the world." 5 For not even His brothers were believing in Him.

This is the request, and at face-value it seems harmless.

John 7:3
3 Therefore His brothers said to Him, "Leave here and go into Judea, so that Your disciples also may see Your works which You are doing."

We know that Jesus is losing followers because His teaching is too hard to hear. If numbers were the measure of success, then Jesus could have easily gotten tremendous crowds of followers. All He would have had to do is feed them and give them miracles; that's all they really wanted. But when Jesus starts teaching truth, they can't handle it, and they are leaving in multitudes.

On the surface it, seems the brothers are simply pleading with Him to go, captivate, and regain those who have walked away. But as we look more closely, we see it is more of a rebuke, and one with improper motives.

---

[1] R. Kent Hughes, *John: That You May Believe*, Preaching the Word (Wheaton, IL: Crossway, 2014), 216.

They had seen the works, but the Word outweighed the works. And so the real issue comes out in verse 4.

John 7:4
4 "For no one does anything in secret when he himself seeks to be known publicly. If You do these things, show Yourself to the world."

They are saying, "If you are the Christ, if you are the political Messiah, then go up and make a name for yourself! Be known!" Just like those in John 6 wanted to make Him king, at this point His brothers have no idea of the purpose for which Jesus came.

The world offers popularity, and the brothers made a very selfish request. But for us, it can be a very tempting request. It reminds me of Jesus in the wilderness, when He was tempted by the devil.

Matthew 4:8
8 The devil took Him to a very high mountain and showed Him all the kingdoms of the world and their glory; 9 and he said to Him, "All these things I will give You, if You fall down and worship me."

The brothers are promoting self-glory, but they're lost and do not understand Jesus and the perfect timing of His last days.

Again, if Jesus just wanted to be popular, that would be easy. The same temptation goes for us today. Recently, one of my dear friends called me and encouraged me to keep preaching the truth, but I do have the option of simply tickling the ear.

The world wants us to worry about being popular and seek the approval of man. But that isn't Jesus' purpose, and it shouldn't be our purpose either. If you have an inner desire to make a name for yourself, be careful. God just may allow it.

They want Jesus to go to Judea, but He has already said that He isn't going (at least the way they want Him to). They wanted Jesus to go for the wrong reasons. Their motives are bad, and the text tells us,

John 7:5
5 For not even His brothers were believing in Him.

It's one thing to be rejected by the world. It's another thing to be rejected by your family.

Many of us know this feeling too well. We have loved ones who don't believe in Christ, and they encourage us to just be accepting of this or that sin so that we are not so offensive. They may say things like, "You could have so many more people who would attend your church if you would just lighten up. What's really wrong with drinking, homosexuality, or women in the pulpit?"

Jesus didn't compromise, and we can't compromise either. He wasn't living a private life. He was working, preaching, and teaching in Galilee. Maybe it wasn't as cosmopolitan or sophisticated as Jerusalem, but souls needed saving there, too.

Crowds are easy to get. We could just host a circus and fill the venue. The brother's problem was that they didn't believe. They were spiritually blind, and it was impossible for them to make wise, gospel-centered decisions.

Maybe you feel that you should be noticed more, perhaps in your workplace or within the ministry you serve, or as a husband who leads and provides for your family or wife who serves her husband and children. Maybe you're the child who works hard for his parents. You want to be recognized and seek popularity.

Let me remind you that Jesus became most popular on the cross. If you want to be known, then die to self and serve God and one day He will say, "Well done." All at the right time.

We have seen the reason and the request, now let's look at the response.

THE RESPONSE

After His brothers revealed their ignorance by rebuking Him for not going, and for questioning His motives, Jesus responds.

John 7:6
6 So Jesus said to them, "My time is not yet here, but your time is always opportune."

Jesus didn't allow their unbelief to drive His actions; rather, He reminds them, "My time is not yet here." This points us to the reality that Jesus knows when He must die, and a public entry into Judea would surely bring that about at the wrong time.

Here the Greek word for "time" is καιρός, which refers to an "opportune moment." This isn't the same Greek word that is used in John 2:4 when John says,

John 2:3–4
3 When the wine ran out, the mother of Jesus said to Him, "They have no wine." 4 And Jesus said to her, "Woman, what does that have to do with us? My hour has not yet come."

The Greek word ὥρα translated as "hour" here refers to a specific time, a certain hour.

Jesus was on God's timetable, there was a specific hour, an opportune moment in time and He followed that specific pattern. He knew that His brothers wanted Him to present Himself in glory to those in the city, but the glorified Christ would come later on the cross. Jesus has different plans, and so He says,

John 7:6
6 So Jesus said to them, "My time is not yet here, but your time is always opportune."

Jesus is saying to His unbelieving brothers, "You're worldly. They are not out to kill you, but they are out to have My head! You can take the trip, be religious, make yourself known, and draw attention to yourself at any time, because you are of this world. I am not."

We see Jesus's train of thought develop more in verse 7.

John 7:7
7 "The world cannot hate you, but it hates Me because I testify of it, that its deeds are evil."

Jesus is essentially saying, "No one is seeking to kill you, because they don't hate you. They don't hate you because, like them, you are lovers of this world."

We have to make sure that as Christians, we are not so loved by the world that we are liked by the world, because we have been warned that we will face problems if we are of Christ.

John 15:18–19
18 "If the world hates you, you know that it has hated Me before it hated you. 19 If you were of the world, the world would love its own; but because you are not of the world, but I chose you out of the world, because of this the world hates you."

Are you loved by the world? I am not suggesting that we should be religious jerks, but simply confirming that we are of the Father.

1 John 2:15
15 Do not love the world nor the things in the world. If anyone loves the world, the love of the Father is not in him.

It begins with transformation.

Romans 12:2
2 And do not be conformed to this world, but be transformed by the renewing of your mind, so that you may prove what the will of God is, that which is good and acceptable and perfect.

The brothers' request is made outside of God's timeline, and the response is cutting. Jesus essentially says, "You have freedom, because God is not your director."

I wonder how many reading this right now are directing their own lives and decisions? How many are building their futures, rather than being moved along by the power of the Holy Spirit?

Jesus' brothers were not hated! If you are hated by the world, it could be because you obey Jesus. Or it could be because you are willing, like Christ, to expose evil in the world.

But if you're seeking popularity from the world, be warned.

Isaiah 5:20
20 Woe to those who call evil good, and good evil; Who substitute darkness for light and light for darkness; Who substitute bitter for sweet and sweet for bitter!

You might gain popularity from the world, but that isn't who you should be trying to please. Now is the time to expose the evil in our world and promote godliness. And the world will hate us for it.

Jesus has a response, and it's simple. He says, "I can't go, because I am a dead man walking, and because I reveal the evil that is in the world. But the world loves you, because like them you don't believe. You're okay with evil, so there is no threat."

And so Jesus' exchange with His brothers concludes,

John 7:8–9
8 "Go up to the feast yourselves; I do not go up to this feast because My time has not yet fully come." 9 Having said these things to them, He stayed in Galilee.

It could be a temptation for some of us to go, right? Applying this to our lives, we have to be careful not to give into godless persuasion. "Oh, just have one little drink. God's not mad." "You can watch that. It won't hurt you." "Text her, flirt just a little, your parents won't know, your spouse will never be aware." "There is no harm in giving that woman a compliment privately, even though you're married to another woman." "Take that job. Abdicate your role as husband or wife for worldly gain."

I love Jesus' verbal response, but I love his actions even more.

John 7:10
10 But when His brothers had gone up to the feast, then He Himself also went up, not publicly, but as if, in secret.

You will not pin Jesus down, but He won't do it on anyone's terms but God's. He wasn't seeking glory from men, but from the Father.

You see, timing is everything! We've looked at the reason, the request, and the response. Finally, we need to understand the reaction.

THE REACTION

Jesus heads up to the Feast of Booths, and going from Jerusalem to Galilee took three days of travel, if you went through Samaria. If you went around Samaria the trip required two additional days of walking.

When He arrives, we come to the realization that the Jews are looking for Jesus. They know He will have to be there, but He is incognito.

John 7:11
11 So the Jews were seeking Him at the feast and were saying, "Where is He?"

He's there. They just can't see Him. And their reaction is to be puzzled about why Jesus the Messiah (or the One who claims to be Messiah) isn't at the feast as required by Jewish law.

As the crowd begins to talk and discuss this, we are told that,

John 7:12
12 There was much grumbling among the crowds concerning Him; some were saying, "He is a good man"; others were saying, "No, on the contrary, He leads the people astray."

Everyone is trying to figure Jesus out. Even today, people talk about Him. Some say, "Oh, He is a good man." Others say, "He is false." But what's interesting is that just as Jesus was present at their discussion, so He is present even today.

Notice the final detail in their reaction. They were doing all of this talking and grumbling, but in verse 13, it says,

John 7:13
13 Yet no one was speaking openly of Him for fear of the Jews.

When you are in a legalistic setting, fear is the driving force. They were not talking openly. Why? Because they were afraid of the leaders of the Jews.

That is a stronghold kind of leadership, and it's destructive to people. There is a lack of reliance on the Holy Spirit, and there's a push for change from us rather than from the Word. These people were unwilling to speak out of fear.

American Christians have become like this about their faith. They are unwilling to speak openly about Christ out of fear, because it's not popular.

Matthew 10:32–34
*32 "Therefore everyone who confesses Me before men, I will also
confess him before My Father who is in heaven. 33 But whoever denies
Me before men, I will also deny him before My Father who is in heaven.
34 Do not think that I came to bring peace on the earth; I did not come
to bring peace, but a sword."*

He came that you might have life, and that your life might be His life,
and that your life might be directed by Him who knows all things.

Remember, timing is everything, and today is the day of salvation.

Romans 10:8–10
*8 But what does it say? "THE WORD IS NEAR YOU, IN YOUR MOUTH AND IN
YOUR HEART"—that is, the word of faith which we are preaching, 9 that if
you confess with your mouth Jesus as Lord and believe in your heart that
God raised Him from the dead, you will be saved; 10 for with the heart a
person believes, resulting in righteousness, and with the mouth he
confesses, resulting in salvation.*

Jesus is on a timetable and He is not swayed by fear of men. He follows
the will of the Father.

The time to glorify God in your life, in your walk, in your ministry, and
in your family is now, so make sure you respond well, unlike those
present at the feast.

If you haven't received Christ, today is the day; if you have, get back to
action in your walk with God.

CHAPTER 6

THE POWER OF PREACHING
John 7:14–18

It has been said that George Whitefield once preached, to a crowd of about 20,000 people, a message that was said to have been heard over two miles away.[1] Two miles, 20,000 people, outside, and no microphone! Can you imagine the volume of that man's voice?

But, compared to the teachings of Christ and the power of the Word, that was nothing. There was never one who could preach more powerfully than Him. When Jesus taught, He shocked the world with His teachings. His words drew men, women, and children to Himself. His teachings also deterred people from coming to Him, and literally pushed them away. That is what powerful preaching does; it pulls and pushes.

The words of Jesus are the very words of God, and the Word of God is living and active.

Hebrews 4:12
12 For the word of God is living and active and sharper than any two-edged sword, and piercing as far as the division of soul and spirit, of both joints and marrow, and able to judge the thoughts and intentions of the heart.

The Word is not only living and active, but it is also transforming and faith-giving.

Romans 10:17
17 Faith comes from hearing, and hearing by the word of Christ.

The Word is living and active, transforming and faith-giving, and it is profitable.

2 Timothy 3:16–17
16 All Scripture is inspired by God and profitable for teaching, for reproof, for correction, for training in righteousness; 17 so that the man of God may be adequate, equipped for every good work.

---

[1] Matt Carter and Josh Wredberg, *Exalting Jesus in John*, Christ-Centered Exposition Commentary (Nashville: B & H Publishing, 2017), 173.

Here in our portion of Scripture today, we find that Jesus, while He came to the Jews' Feast of Booths undercover, is about to expose Himself, and to do so in a most powerful manner.

I couldn't help asking the question, "What made Jesus switch so quickly?" I find it interesting that, after what just happened, Jesus is suddenly about to reveal Himself in His own timing and within His own methods.

Jesus, if you recall, was asked by His unbelieving brothers to journey up to the Feast of Booths as the Jewish people would travel. They desired that Jesus go up and make Himself known among the Jewish people, but Jesus made it clear that it wasn't the proper time. Rather, Jesus went up to the feast undercover, when it was the right time.

His purpose is, and always will be, to glorify God (not, primarily, to draw attention to Himself). We will see this very idea within our text, because the power of preaching is always about glorifying God. It's always making known to the world what God has said.

So, without delay let us jump into our text.

John 7:14–18
14 But when it was now the midst of the feast Jesus went up into the temple, and began to teach. 15 The Jews then were astonished, saying, "How has this man become learned, having never been educated?" 16 So Jesus answered them and said, "My teaching is not Mine, but His who sent Me. 17 If anyone is willing to do His will, he will know of the teaching, whether it is of God or whether I speak from Myself. 18 He who speaks from himself seeks his own glory; but He who is seeking the glory of the One who sent Him, He is true, and there is no unrighteousness in Him."

There are three things we must consider today as we approach this text. Frist, we must consider the question; second, we must consider the promise; and third, we must consider the principle.

THE QUESTION

Remember, Jesus is there in Jerusalem at the Feast of Booths. It's an exciting time of celebration and remembrance, and Jesus has gone up after the brothers. He is walking around, hearing all that is happening, and we are told that He makes a transition.

John 7:14
14 But when it was now the midst of the feast Jesus went up into the temple, and began to teach.

This makes no sense on the surface, because He has already said in verses 8–9,

John 7:8–9
8 "Go up to the feast yourselves; I do not go up to this feast because My time has not yet fully come." 9 Having said these things to them, He stayed in Galilee.

But then He goes. The message is that He intended to go, just differently than expected. Now He is here, and we read that,

John 7:11–13
11 So the Jews were seeking Him at the feast and were saying, "Where is He?" 12 There was much grumbling among the crowds concerning Him; some were saying, "He is a good man"; others were saying, "No, on the contrary, He leads the people astray." 13 Yet no one was speaking openly of Him for fear of the Jews.

What a great opportunity for Jesus to reveal truth to these people. They have so many questions, so many misconceptions, as to who He really is.

John 7:14
14 But when it was now the midst of the feast, Jesus went up into the temple, and began to teach.

Is our heart like the heart of Christ, always ready and desiring to share the truth? If this is the heart of Jesus, it should be our heart as well.

Have you taken the opportunity, even in an uncomfortable place, to hold fast to preaching the truth, teaching the truth, and uplifting Christian doctrine?

I saw it this week at our local VBS. People were faithfully preaching the gospel to children. They were teaching them about Christ, and they were sharing with them the hope of Jesus. The power of preaching and teaching is found in the Word of God, and here, Jesus Christ, the very Word of God that became flesh, isn't going to miss this opportunity to preach.

So we are told that He begins to teach. Here, the word for "teach," comes from the Greek word, διδάσκω, which means, "to tell someone what to do, tell, instruct; to provide instruction in a formal or informal setting, teach."[2]

I love the response Jesus gets from the people in the temple as He teaches.

John 7:15
15 The Jews then were astonished,

The power of preaching results in astonishment. They are bewildered, stunned, and captivated. They couldn't believe how well He handled the Scriptures. We are not told what Jesus taught on, but only that He taught, and that what He taught impressed them greatly.

As a result of them being astonished by the preaching and teaching of Jesus, consider the question that arises as a result. The text says,

John 7:15
15 The Jews then were astonished, saying, "How has this man become learned, having never been educated?"

This is a powerful question. The religious leaders of this day took much pride in their educational system. For the scribes and the Pharisees, it would have been unthinkable that a man who had not passed through their educational system would ever have the power to preach like Jesus. "He isn't schooled to handle the Law," they thought. But Jesus is something special. He teaches something special, and He handles it in such a special way, that they ask the question, "How did Jesus get so smart?"

Most would have to lean on their education as an explanation for why they are good at whatever they are doing. Some would say today, "He has the ability to preach, because He has certificates or a degree from this

---

[2] William Arndt, Frederick William Danker, and Walter Bauer, *A Greek-English Lexicon of the New Testament and Other Early Christian literature*, 3rd ed. (Chicago: University of Chicago Press, 2000), 241.

or that place." But Jesus had nothing from the rabbinic school of Old Testament Law. Jesus doesn't have a degree on the wall.

Education (while it has some importance) isn't the standard by which to determine how someone got so wise. If that were the case, then Jesus would be like they expected—uneducated—because He wasn't trained by them.

The power of preaching isn't founded in a seminary degree. It isn't found in your certificate, and we have to make sure we don't look straight to the level of education to determine if someone is able to teach well. The power of preaching is in the Word of God.

We must make sure, as churches and ministries or even teachers of the Word in general, that we don't become proud., thinking that we are the only church, person, or ministry that can teach the gospel, that can handle sound doctrine, or that can promote solid biblical theology. If one is willing to preach with the power of God's Word, anyone can experience the power of preaching and teaching.

To their question, "How has this man become learned, having never been educated?" Jesus could have said, "Because I'm God," but He doesn't. Rather, Jesus, who is validating the power of preaching and teaching, answers them much differently, and with an answer which should perk up all of our ears, as followers of Christ.

John 7:16
16 So Jesus answered them and said, "My teaching is not Mine, but His who sent Me.

Jesus is saying, "What I teach isn't some fabrication made by man, nor taught by a school. It's not mine, but God's!"

I love how He simply doesn't take credit. The schools I attended certainly challenged me—they invested into me and helped me sharpen my tools—but it is by God's grace and His revealing truth that I have learned and grown as a pastor.

Paul said the same.

Galatians 1:11–12
11 For I would have you know, brethren, that the gospel which was preached by me is not according to man. 12 For I neither received it from man, nor was I taught it, but I received it through a revelation of Jesus Christ.

If we are going to experience the power of preaching and the power of teaching, it will always begin with God's Word in us and through us, giving God glory (which is man's sole purpose).

If you want to be wise, know the Word of God. You don't need a seminary degree to know God's Word. You need a Bible. Much of our problem is that we don't preach God's Word, but instead, we preach "feel good" messages, stories, and illustrations that don't challenge or change anyone. Only the Word can do that.

It's easy to teach people from our experiences, emotions, and everything else, but those aren't the examples Jesus gives us. We see this in John 7:14–16.

John 7:14–16
14 But when it was now the midst of the feast Jesus went up into the temple, and began to teach. 15 The Jews then were astonished, saying, "How has this man become learned, having never been educated?" 16 So Jesus answered them and said, "My teaching is not Mine, but His who sent Me."

There is power in preaching, when, and if, we will preach and teach the Word of God.

It takes time. It takes sacrifice. It takes investment. And if you aren't willing to put the work in, then don't teach, because it will be powerless. Let the Word of God grab your heart. Let the Word of God penetrate your soul first. Pour over, seek after, meditate on, marinate in, the Word of God, and then, preach. Preach with the power of God's living and active, life-giving Word. There is power in preaching, if your preaching is, indeed, like Christ's: from the Word of God.

Let the Spirit of God work through the Word of God, so that when we do preach and teach, it will honor God, glorify God, and point people to Christ.

Not only must we consider the question, but second, we must consider the promise.

THE PROMISE

Jesus delivers a promise in His response to the Jewish people here in this temple, during the Feast of Booths. We see Him continue speaking in verse 17.

John 7:17
17 "If anyone is willing to do His will, he will know of the teaching, whether it is of God or whether I speak from Myself."

Are we willing to do His will? Are you willing to submit to the Father's will for your life? Are you willing to follow God where He guides? Are you willing to submit to the roles which God has given you?

The Old Testament is full of stories of people who achieved amazing accomplishments. But we're so familiar with these stories, that we may overlook the real message: that God called them to faithful service, to obey His will for their lives. Are you like Moses or like Daniel, willing to obey God's will?

Romans gives us some insight into how to do this.

Romans 12:2
2 And do not be conformed to this world, but be transformed by the renewing of your mind, so that you may prove what the will of God is, that which is good and acceptable and perfect.

John Piper writes that, "Paul is referring to God's will of command. I say this for at least two reasons. One is that God does not intend for us to know most of his sovereign will ahead of time. 'The secret things belong to the Lord our God, but the things that are revealed belong to us' (Deut 29:29). If you want to know the future details of God's will of decree, you don't want a renewed mind, you want a crystal ball...The other reason I say that the will of God in Romans 12:2 is God's will of command and not his will of decree is that the phrase "by testing you may discern" implies that we should approve of the will of God and then obediently do it."[3]

---

[3] John Piper, "What Is the Will of God and How Do We Know It?" *Desiring God,*

It begins with being in the Word, because this is how God speaks to us today—through His living and active Word.

In John 7:17, there is a promise tucked in there.

John 7:17
17 "If anyone is willing to do His will, he will know of the teaching, whether it is of God or whether I speak from Myself."

If you are willing to do the will of God, from the smallest of things, to the greatest of things, God promises that you will know His teaching is true. The key to the power of preaching and the power of teaching is still the power of God's Word—God's truth!

The key to recognizing God's truth is not found in a book. It's not taught in a seminary. It's not found in a good podcast. It lies within a heart willing to obey the will of God, Who speaks through His living and active Word.

We see all kinds of people in Scripture, but there are two kinds that I think are worth examining. One is the kind of people who are willing to sit and submit to the teachings of Jesus, and the other is the kind of people who want to argue with Jesus's teachings. That second group is the Jewish leaders. They are unable to discern about what Jesus is claiming, "whether it is of God or whether I speak from Myself," because they are unwilling to do His will.

Are you following God's will, or are you fighting God's will? The answer to this is what determines whether we are able to know and receive what God has taught.

We must consider the promise. The assurance promised in this verse is available to all true followers of Christ—to all believers in Him. This confidence comes from, and through, the Holy Spirit who dwells in you, to confirm His truth.

We must consider the question, the promise, and finally, we must consider the principle.

August 22, 2004, https://www.desiringgod.org/messages/what-is-the-will-of-god-and-how-do-we-know-it.

THE PRINCIPLE

The power of preaching drives a question. The question drives a promise. The promise promotes a principle. The principle is this: that, just as we are to commit to doing the will of God, we are to promote the glory of God.

If you are going to experience the power of preaching, or the power of teaching, you must be promoting the glory of God, because all the power comes from God above, through His written and revealed Word.

If you want to promote anything other than the glory of God, you will not only miss out on the power of preaching, but you will also prove to be a false teacher.

John 7:18
18 "He who speaks from himself seeks his own glory; but He who is seeking the glory of the One who sent Him, He is true, and there is no unrighteousness in Him."

First, if you are going to honor God and experience the power of preaching, you must not speak from yourself. Your message must be driven by the Word of God, not by the work of you.

One characteristic of false teachers is that they speak with their own authority. In a day where the prosperity gospel is rampant, where unsound doctrine flows from the pulpit, and where people speak from the convictions of their opinions, we must make sure that what we preach and teach has power from the Word of God and not from the word of man.

Here is a reminder from 2 Peter 2:1.

2 Peter 2:1
1 But false prophets also arose among the people, just as there will also be false teachers among you, who will secretly introduce destructive heresies, even denying the Master who bought them, bringing swift destruction upon themselves.

These people have been invaded by false teachers, who have been involved in a faulty system of legalistic methodology. They are crowded by a bunch of people who speak on their own authority.

We can debate doctrinal matters, but all that matters is the book, chapter, and verse of the Word of God, not your own opinion, nor your own authority. There is no power in your own opinion and authority; at least, no transforming power from above.

Because of this, we must preach with power from above, from the Word of God, and not from the authority of man.

John 7:18
18 "He who speaks from himself seeks his own glory;"

The second principle is that we should be promoting the glory of God, not of man. The desire of Christ is that they get past the desire to glorify themselves, and rather, bring honor to God. Because what is the chief end of man? The "Westminster Shorter Catechism" begins by reminding us that, "Man's chief end is to glorify God and to enjoy him forever."[4]

1 Corinthians 10:31
31 Whether, then, you eat or drink or whatever you do, do all to the glory of God.

If you are going to experience the power of preaching and the power of teaching, it is essential that you do it to the glory of God, and that you seek not the approval of man. The only way for you to do that to the glory of God is for you to preach the Word of God, which promotes the glory of God.

Romans 11:36
36 For from Him and through Him and to Him are all things. To Him be the glory forever. Amen.

On the contrary, a false teacher is one who does just the opposite.

---

[4] *Westminster Shorter Catechism*, The Westminster Standard, accessed March 24, 2023, https://thewestminsterstandard.org/westminster-shorter-catechism/.

John 7:18
18 "He who speaks from himself seeks his own glory; but He who is seeking the glory of the One who sent Him, He is true, and there is no unrighteousness in Him."

Our example is Jesus, and Jesus didn't come to gain popularity. Jesus didn't come to receive His own glory for Himself. Jesus didn't come to speak on His own behalf.

John 12:49
49 "For I did not speak on My own initiative, but the Father Himself who sent Me has given Me a commandment as to what to say and what to speak."

Jesus says, "Instead of bringing glory to Myself, I promote God the Father, because I am the true One, in whom there is no unrighteousness."

John 5:44
44 "How can you believe, when you receive glory from one another, and you do not seek the glory that is from the one and only God?"

In everything we do, from preaching to parenting, we must stop seeking glory for ourselves. Stop trying to be good enough and putting your efforts on the altar of justification. Rather, trust God today, and place your faith in Christ, so that you can have a personal relationship with Christ.

Maybe you're reading today, and you have that, and you feel powerless in your ability. Your power is in the Word. And when God works and changes hearts, it will be through the power of His Word. You preach the Word, and allow God, through the power of the Holy Spirit, to work in the hearts of people all around you.

CHAPTER 7

THE HEART OF HYPOCRISY
John 7:19–24

In the last chapter, we looked at what we called the "power of preaching." And Jesus is going to continue teaching in the temple during the Feast of Booths (known to some as the Feast of Tabernacles), but He is now teaching about hypocrisy.

John 7:19–24
19 "Did not Moses give you the Law, and yet none of you carries out the Law? Why do you seek to kill Me?" 20 The crowd answered, "You have a demon! Who seeks to kill You?" 21 Jesus answered them, "I did one deed, and you all marvel. 22 For this reason Moses has given you circumcision (not because it is from Moses, but from the fathers), and on the Sabbath you circumcise a man. 23 If a man receives circumcision on the Sabbath so that the Law of Moses will not be broken, are you angry with Me because I made an entire man well on the Sabbath? 24 Do not judge according to appearance, but judge with righteous judgment."

There are three things to see as we work our way through the text: the heart of hypocrisy is disobedience, disillusionment, and dishonor.

THE HEART OF HYPOCRISY IS DISOBEDIENCE

Jesus continues His teaching in the temple, and He continues by asking two questions. In John 7:19, the text says,

John 7:19
19 "Did not Moses give you the Law, and yet none of you carries out the Law? Why do you seek to kill Me?"

The point Jesus is making here is simple. He says, "Did not Moses give you the law?" It's a rhetorical question. He is making a claim by asking a question. He is simply saying, "Moses gave you the Law, but none of you obey it!"

The fact is that, prior to this, they wanted to draw attention to themselves as being Law abiders, when they were not obeying the Law. That disobedience is the heart of hypocrisy.

All hypocrisy is, "behavior that contradicts what one claims to believe or feel, *especially* the false assumption of an appearance of virtue or religion."[1] Hypocrisy is not practicing what you preach.

Part of the reason it's so hard to call sin out in the lives of others is that, deep down, we have our own secret sins. Calling a sin a "sin" in the lives of others convicts our hearts, because we all have things no one else can see.

But Jesus can see into the depths of these men's souls, because Christ Jesus, in the form of a man, is the all-knowing God.

One of the hardest parts of the Christian life, is to obey what we know to be true, namely, to do what we know to be right, and to hold back from what we know to be wrong. But, like them, when we disobey the Lord's will for our lives, we too become hypocrites. And when we do what we know isn't right, we exemplify hypocrisy, and we have a negative impact on the gospel.

These Jewish leaders and the people in the temple have been hypocrites. They have been seeking self-glory. They dress in a way that points people to themselves, rather than to God. As they are seeking their own glory, they fail to believe the Christ, as we are reminded in John 5:44.

John 5:44
44 "How can you believe, when you receive glory from one another and you do not seek the glory that is from the one and only God?"

They wanted to be known as righteous people of God. It was their whole system. But Christ calls them out for what they really were, in Matthew 23:27.

---

[1] *Merriam Webster Online*, s.v. "Hypocrisy, *n.*," accessed March 24, 2023, https://www.merriam-webster.com/dictionary/hypocrisy.

Matthew 23:27
27 "Woe to you, scribes and Pharisees, hypocrites! For you are like whitewashed tombs which on the outside appear beautiful, but inside they are full of dead men's bones and all uncleanness."

Jesus, by questioning them, is revealing to them, and to us, the reality that the heart of hypocrisy is disobedience.

So Jesus asks in John 7:19,

John 7:19a
19 "Did not Moses give you the Law, and yet none of you carries out the Law?"

Then, in that same verse, He inserts the next interesting question.

John 7:19b
19 "Why do you seek to kill Me?"

Jesus is saying, "If you have been given the Law of Moses, you should know that murder isn't lawful!" For both Jesus and His debaters, the will of God is revealed in the Law.[2]

Psalm 40:8
8 I delight to do Your will, O my God; Your Law is within my heart.

"So," Jesus asks, "if you are Law followers, if you are clean and pure for doing all that the Law says, then, why do you seek to kill Me? You have the Law, and yet you try to kill the only One that can obey the Law, God in flesh! You're the guilty ones! If anyone should be being killed here, it should be you, not the Son of God, who is perfectly clean on the inside and the outside."

But they are willing to disobey the Law in order to kill Jesus, which we know they have been planning since chapter 5. This is what He will address next.

---

[2] D. A. Carson, *The Gospel According to John*, Pillar New Testament Commentary (Grand Rapids, MI: Eerdmans, 1991), 313.

The warning here is that, if you and I are not careful, we will justify just about anything to make ourselves look good, righteous, and holier than what we are. Many, like them, will seek the Law unto salvation, and will look to their deeds as to what saves them. If you believe that your "lack" of sinning gets you closer to salvation, then you are wrong.

Your "lack" of sinning gets you not one inch closer to salvation. Maybe you haven't had a drink, haven't done drugs, or haven't lusted after people, places, or things. Maybe you haven't been bitter towards a loved one that has hurt you, and maybe you haven't gossiped lately. Maybe you have never killed anyone.

But even if you are a good person, you are not perfect, and you were born into sin. Your sins have made a separation between you and God, and Jesus Christ alone is your solution to salvation, for there is no other Name given unto men, by which we must be saved. No one can keep this Law. We are all equally Law-breakers.

The whole Jewish system was built on keeping the Law of Moses, so that people could acquire salvation based on carefully following the rules. Here we see that Jesus is the only One who could do all that the Law required, yet He is the very one they are seeking to kill. They are willing to break the Law, and therefore disobey the will of God; because of this, they can't see the truth. If you remember, Jesus said in John 7:17,

John 7:17
17 "If anyone is willing to do His will, he will know of the teaching, whether it is of God or whether I speak from Myself."

The only way they will know the truth is if they are willing to do His will. But they haven't done His will, and they don't believe. So,

John 7:20
20 The crowd answered, "You have a demon! Who seeks to kill You?"

They act as if the leaders are not seeking to kill Jesus, but it's not a well-kept secret. John 7:13 reminds us that the crowds knew something was going on, because they were talking about Jesus and who He was.

John 7:13
13 Yet no one was speaking openly of Him for fear of the Jews.

They were cowards before the religious leaders. The leaders knew, and it seems that many of the crowd had heard. Look at verse 25.

John 7:25
25 So some of the people of Jerusalem were saying, "Is this not the man whom they are seeking to kill?"

They knew, yet they simply claimed, "You have a demon!" That statement would have been understood the same as saying, "You're out of your mind!" or, "You're a mad man!"

These leaders and this crowd were unwilling to believe Jesus, and the result is disobedience. The heart of hypocrisy is disobedience, and their willingness to break the Law shows the depths of their sin.

The heart of hypocrisy is disobedience, and, if we are not careful, we will do the same. We will gossip and break others down, so that we can build ourselves up. We will do whatever it takes, claiming that it's, "all in the name of Jesus," yet living hypocritical lives all the more. And if we are not careful, we will try to do everything in our power to obtain and maintain our entrance into heaven, by holding fast to the Law. But the warning there in Galatians 3:10, is that,

Galatians 3:10
10 For as many as are of the works of the Law are under a curse; for it is written, "Cursed is everyone who does not abide by all things written in the book of the law, to perform them."

It is vital that we understand that no one is justified by the Law before God, and that is evident, for Scripture goes on to say, in Galatians 3:11,

Galatians 3:11
11 Now that no one is justified by the Law before God is evident; for, "The righteous man shall live by faith."

That faith is in Christ.

Galatians 2:21
21 "I do not nullify the grace of God, for if righteousness comes through the Law, then Christ died needlessly."

The problem is that no religious system, and no religious methods, will get you, or anyone else, into heaven. Living as if religious systems or religious methods could get you into heaven just makes you a hypocrite as well.

Not only is the heart of hypocrisy a willingness on our part to disobey what we know to be true of God and His will for our lives; but the heart of hypocrisy is also disillusionment.

THE HEART OF HYPOCRISY IS DISILLUSIONMENT

Jesus continues this opportunity of publicly teaching in the temple. Notice that they asked the questions, but Jesus refrains from responding to their questions directly. Rather, in verse 21, He responds differently,

John 7:21
21 Jesus answered them, "I did one deed, and you all marvel."

Again, Jesus is about to get to the heart of hypocrisy. He isn't playing their games, and He isn't following their lead. He has an objective, and it is to reveal their disillusionment—which reveals again, the heart of their hypocrisy.

These people think it's okay to break God's Law. They have justified it in their minds, and therefore, they have become disillusioned, because they are under the curse of the Law.

It's what we all do when we act hypocritically. We do what we know we shouldn't, and somehow we disillusion ourselves just enough to commit and follow through with it. When we follow through with hypocrisy, all we are doing is showing how disillusioned we are. We haven't considered the consequences.

King David didn't consider the consequences of his affair with Bathsheba; rather, he was disillusioned. He thought that he would gain so much more. However, he experienced disappointment instead, because it didn't work out the way he thought it would.

The Lord denounced the hypocrisy of the people during the days of the prophet, Isaiah, in Isaiah 29:13.

Isaiah 29:13
13 Then the Lord said, "Because this people draw near with their words And honor Me with their lip service, But they remove their hearts far from Me, And their reverence for Me consists of tradition learned by rote,"

In Matthew 7:3–5, we see Jesus deal with the hypocrisy of His day.

Matthew 7:3–5
3 "Why do you look at the speck that is in your brother's eye, but do not notice the log that is in your own eye? 4 Or how can you say to your brother, 'Let me take the speck out of your eye,' and behold, the log is in your own eye? 5 You hypocrite, first take the log out of your own eye, and then you will see clearly to take the speck out of your brother's eye."

Jesus is in the process of revealing their hypocrisy, and it's not a good thing. Jesus is talking here in John 7:21 about something He did, at which the people all marveled. He is using this as an illustration to show them that they are breaking their own set of rules. He is showing them that they are taking liberty to act outside their own system and justifying their actions simultaneously.

We are not told yet which event Jesus is referring to. We are simply told in verse 21 that He did one deed at which they marveled. Jesus could well be referring back to John 5:1–17, in which He healed the man who had been paralyzed for thirty-eight years. That one work evoked astonishment, but not the astonishment that leads to praise. Rather, it evokes the astonishment that someone would actually tell another to carry his mat on the Sabbath day, openly breaking the accepted norms for Sabbath conduct.[3]

Jesus continues by stating,

John 7:22
22 "For this reason Moses has given you circumcision (not because it is from Moses, but from the fathers), and on the Sabbath you circumcise a man."

Jesus has just called these men out for breaking the law of Moses. They are disillusioned, thinking it's okay to break the Sabbath if it's for

---

[3] Carson, *The Gospel According to John*, 314.

circumcision. So "Jesus refused to be categorized as a breaker of the law in the same way that the rabbis argued they were not breaking the law when they were circumcising male babies on the eighth day, even though the day would be the Sabbath."[4]

If you're under the Law, you're under the curse of the Law, and you must follow the Law to a "T." If you break that Law, then you are a transgressor of the Law.

It's freeing when you see someone trust Christ and come out of that legalistic methodology.

John 7:23
23 "If a man receives circumcision on the Sabbath so that the Law of Moses will not be broken, are you angry with Me because I made an entire man well on the Sabbath?"

When Jesus says that, "If a man receives circumcision on the Sabbath so that the Law of Moses will not be broken," He's essentially saying, "If it's okay to do circumcision on the Sabbath and it is not considered breaking the Law, then why are you angry with Me because I made an entire man well on the Sabbath?"

They are disillusioned, and they are being hypocritical. The heart of hypocrisy is disillusionment. If you and I aren't careful, we will think it's okay to do what we think others shouldn't do, and then we will be the ones to call them out when we're just as much to blame.

These men are angry to the point of wanting to kill the Son of God because He made a man well on the Sabbath, and yet they are breaking this same system they accuse Him of transgressing. Under the system of the Law, they are breaking the rules. Under the law of grace, Jesus isn't. The only way they could think this way and have no guilt is through disillusionment.

Are you disillusioned today? All of us need to repent and turn to Christ, to His grace and mercy. We can't keep living as disillusioned people, living hypocritical lives.

---

[4] Gerald L. Borchert, *John 1–11: An Exegetical and Theological Exposition of Holy Scripture*, The New American Commentary, vol. 25 (Nashville: Broadman & Holman, 1996), 285).

1 John 1:9
9 If we confess our sins, He is faithful and righteous to forgive us our sins and to cleanse us from all unrighteousness.

We have seen that the heart of hypocrisy is disobedience and disillusionment, and finally we see that the heart of hypocrisy is dishonor.

THE HEART OF HYPOCRISY IS DISHONOR

No one likes to be dishonored. No one likes to have false judgments lodged against them. Not Jesus, not the Pharisees, and not you and me. But when we are acting like hypocrites, it naturally dishonors someone, because there are false judgments taking place.

It is important to note here that sin is sin, and it will always be sin. Call sin, "sin," but stop being the judge as to where one will spend eternity. For example, it is not hypocrisy to teach that drunkenness is a sin, unless the one teaching against drunkenness gets drunk every weekend. That would be hypocrisy.

Jesus is about to make a statement here that will drive that idea home again. He says,

John 7:24
24 "Do not judge according to appearance, but judge with righteous judgment."

Don't judge according to appearance. It doesn't work out most of the time. You might get lucky every now and again and nail one down, but most of the time you have no clue. Judge the sin, the action of it, yes; but let God be their Judge.

These Jews are making a judgment against Jesus. One commentator stated, "Jesus's appeal is more personal, eschatological and redemptive. They have misconstrued His character by a fundamentally flawed set of deductions from Old Testament Law, an approach that turns out to be superficial, far too committed to 'mere appearances.' If their approach to God's will were one of faith, they would soon discern that Jesus is not a

Sabbath-breaker, but the One who fulfills both Sabbath and circumcision."[5]

Those that will take that admonishment and put it to practice will soon see that He isn't some false, floundering, mad man. Rather, those that will continue to lift up and exalt Christ will find Him to be who He claims to be, and that is the Lord Jesus Christ, God in flesh.

So let's be careful when we find ourselves passing judgment on others. It's so easy to do. It's really hard to make a righteous judgment, because there is no one who is righteous, not even one (Rom 3:10). Only Christ knows the hearts of men. God alone is all-knowing.

Therefore, don't let hypocrisy creep in. It comes in through disobedience, disillusionment, and dishonor!

None of these help your holiness. They play no part in your salvation, and they get you no closer to God. The Jews missed who Christ was. Don't miss who Christ is today.

They brought judgment on the One who would pay for their judgment. Do you know Him? He is perfect, sinless, and wants all of us to know that this legalism isn't the way of salvation. He wants all of us to know that He is the Bread of Life and He is the Giver of Life! And if you have never trusted in Him, let today be the day of salvation.

---

[5] Carson, *The Gospel According to John*, 316.

CHAPTER 8

WHO DO YOU SAY THAT I AM?
John 7:25–31

I have entitled this chapter, "Who Do You Say That I Am?" This is the question that drives our passage of Scripture today. It was the question of that day, and it still is the crucial question for us, 2,000 years later. It's the inquiry, the examination, and the debate they had in the days of Jesus ("Who do you say that I am?"), and it is still the driving debate of our day ("Who is Jesus?").

For starters, it was the opinion of Herod Antipas that Jesus was John the Baptist.

Matthew 14:1–2
1 At that time Herod the tetrarch heard the news about Jesus, 2 and said to his servants, "This is John the Baptist; he has risen from the dead, and that is why miraculous powers are at work in him."

In Malachi 4:5, it is written,

Malachi 4:5
5 "Behold, I am going to send you Elijah the prophet before the coming of the great and terrible day of the LORD."

So when the disciples were asked the question, "Who do you say that I am?", some believed that Christ was Elijah (as destined to return before the appearance of Messiah). Some were of the opinion that this Christ was Jeremiah, and others believed Jesus was a prophet. In John 4:25, the woman at the well missed who Jesus was.

In this chapter alone, there is mass confusion as to who Jesus is.

John 7:11–12
11 So the Jews were seeking Him at the feast and were saying, "Where is He?" 12 There was much grumbling among the crowds concerning Him; some were saying, "He is a good man"; others were saying, "No, on the contrary, He leads the people astray."

John 7:20
The crowd answered, "You have a demon! Who seeks to kill You?"

John 7:40
40 Some of the people therefore, when they heard these words, were saying, "This certainly is the Prophet."

Verse, after verse, after verse, shows again the confusion over, "Who is Jesus?"

Almost every major religion teaches that Jesus was a prophet, or a good teacher, or a godly man. But the problem with that is that the Bible tells us differently. The Bible tells us that Jesus was infinitely more than a prophet, substantially more than a good teacher, and significantly more than a godly man. Yes, the Bible teaches that He is so much more.

Three things stand out in this portion of Scripture. First, notice the confusion of the people; second, the clarification of the teacher; and finally, the conviction of the hearers.

THE CONFUSION OF THE PEOPLE

John 7:25–27
25 So some of the people of Jerusalem were saying, "Is this not the man whom they are seeking to kill? 26 Look, He is speaking publicly, and they are saying nothing to Him. The rulers do not really know that this is the Christ, do they? 27 However, we know where this man is from; but whenever the Christ may come, no one knows where He is from."

This text shows more people in confusion. Jesus has just finished a lesson on the heart of hypocrisy, so as He is teaching them about making righteous judgments, they begin talking and showing their misperceptions about who Jesus is.

John 7:25
25 So some of the people of Jerusalem were saying, "Is this not the man whom they are seeking to kill?"

It seems within the context that Jesus is still teaching in the temple, and the people who asked in verse 20, "Who seeks to kill You?", are now asking, "Is this not the man whom they are seeking to kill?"

These people are confused. But they are not confused only because of who Christ is at this point, but because of the hesitation of the Jewish leaders in doing something about this man.

Their first confusion comes in their understanding of Jesus as a man. In verse 25, they said, "Is this not the man whom they are seeking to kill?"

The propositional statement of the whole Book of John, the book's main idea, is found in John 20:31.

John 20:31
31 but these have been written so that you may believe that Jesus is the Christ, the Son of God; and that believing you may have life in His name.

These people are confused as to the person of Christ, but they are also confused as to the persistence of the Jewish leaders.

John 7:25–26
25 "Is this not the man whom they are seeking to kill? 26 Look, He is speaking publicly, and they are saying nothing to Him."

They are confused because these Jewish leaders have been seeking to kill Him since John 5:18, when it said,

John 5:18
18 For this reason therefore the Jews were seeking all the more to kill Him, because He not only was breaking the Sabbath, but also was calling God His own Father, making Himself equal with God.

The people are confused because the Jewish leaders wanted to kill Jesus, and they have been pursuing Him but are not doing anything now, even though they have Jesus right in front of them.

John 7:26
26 "Look, He is speaking publicly, and they are saying nothing to Him."

It would be like a false teacher walking into the pulpit on a Sunday morning and us doing nothing about it. Our actions would speak in huge ways as to what we thought about the one speaking.

The conclusion the people come to is,

John 7:26
"The rulers do not really know that this is the Christ, do they?"

Since actions speak in huge ways, the people are essentially saying, "Jesus is speaking, teaching, preaching, revealing truth, and opening the Word, and these rulers are not saying a word? Is it possible that they, indeed, do not know that this is the Christ?"

That would be the only proper conclusion.

If the rulers aren't saying anything to Jesus, but are hearing and listening, and are not acting, then He must be the Christ. Otherwise, the rulers would seize Him and take Him hostage. So the people could only assume that, because the rulers weren't capturing Him, maybe He was truly the Christ.

The heart of the issue is revealed in verse 27. The possibility that these men are not following through with taking Jesus hostage because they know Him to be the Christ, the Messiah, and the Son of God, fades away because of their faulty understanding of the Christ.

We must not make this same mistake.

Their hunch, their suspicion, and their intuition tells them that this may be the Christ, because the leaders are listening, learning, and not doing a thing about this Man. But as soon as they take this into consideration, their faulty understanding of Christ causes their closeness to be cast away. "No sooner has the suggestion been ventilated than it is dismissed."[1]

All of that neat evidence goes out the window, because they claim to know something when they say,

John 7:27
27 "However, we know where this man is from; but whenever the Christ may come, no one knows where He is from."

---

[1] D. A. Carson, *The Gospel According to John*, Pillar New Testament Commentary (Grand Rapids, MI: Eerdmans, 1991), 317.

I love what A. W. Tozer said: "We can prove our position by the Scriptures; and if any man would admit the authority of the Word of God, we can show how the Jesus of the New Testament came according to the Old Testament Scriptures and walked in all the ways pointed out for Him thousands of years before He was born. He appeared at a certain time, in a certain place and moved with the fine precision of the most expensive watch. Everything happened as God Almighty in the Old Testament prophesied."[2]

These men are mistaken. Their faith is built on that which is faulty.

Of course, the Word of God does state where the Messiah would be born and where He would be raised. One location aligns with the prophecy foretold by Micah, proclaiming that the Christ would be born in Bethlehem.

Micah 5:2
2 "But as for you, Bethlehem Ephrathah, Too little to be among the clans of Judah, From you One will go forth for Me to be ruler in Israel. His goings forth are from long ago, From the days of eternity."

Matthew 2:4–6
4 Gathering together all the chief priests and scribes of the people, he inquired of them where the Messiah was to be born. 5 They said to him, "In Bethlehem of Judea; for this is what has been written by the prophet: 6 'And you, Bethlehem, land of Judah, Are by no means least among the leaders of Judah; For out of you shall come forth a Ruler Who will shepherd My people Israel.'"

Their confusion comes from a lack of understanding. They might not know, but God knows. Christ knows. They keep saying, "This man," or, "This man," or, "This man." Here is God in flesh, and they miss it. They miss that Christ is in the beginning with God, that He is God, and that the Word became flesh (John 1).

They miss that Jesus is the creator of the universe, which we know to be true in Colossians 1:15–17.

---

[2] A. W. Tozer, *And He Dwelt Among Us: Teachings from the Gospel of John*, ed. James L. Snyder (Bloomington, MN: Bethany House Publishers, 2009), 100.

Colossians 1:15–17
15 He is the image of the invisible God, the firstborn of all creation. 16 For by Him all things were created, both in the heavens and on earth, visible and invisible, whether thrones or dominions or rulers or authorities—all things have been created through Him and for Him. 17 He is before all things, and in Him all things hold together.

They miss Him from the Psalms.

Psalms 33:6
6 By the word of the LORD the heavens were made, And by the breath of His mouth all their host.

They miss Him from Isaiah.

Isaiah 42:5–6
5 Thus says God the LORD, Who created the heavens and stretched them out, Who spread out the earth and its offspring, Who gives breath to the people on it, spirit to those who walk in it,
6 "I am the LORD, I have called You in righteousness, I will also hold You by the hand and watch over You, And I will appoint You as a covenant to the people, a light to the nations!"

They miss it from the Book of Hebrews.

Hebrews 11:3
3 By faith we understand that the worlds were prepared by the word of God, so that what is seen was not made out of things which are visible.

This Jesus, who they claim is only a man, is God Himself, in flesh, the creator of the heavens and earth, the sustainer of nations, the protector of salvation, the provider for His creation, the Alpha and the Omega, the beginning and the end, the just and the justifier. He is more than a simple-minded man. He is the One who has come to conquer death, on behalf of all humanity.

These men are blind, and they can't see. They are dead men walking. Martyn Lloyd-Jones said it well: "Strangely enough, the Christian gospel—let me say this with reverence, lest I be misunderstood—the Christian gospel does not even start with the Lord Jesus Christ. It starts with God the Father. The Bible starts with God the Father always, everywhere, and we must do the same, because that is the order in the blessed Trinity: God the Father, God the Son, God the Holy Spirit."[3]

This is God the Son. And yet, they are confused, lost, and in desperate need of deliverance. We can also read this as Jesus asking us directly today, "Who do you say that I am?"

That man, Christ Jesus, the Son of God, is about to reveal Himself once again. We have seen the confusion of the people, and now we turn to the clarification of the Teacher.

THE CLARIFICATION OF THE TEACHER

After all this confusion, Jesus is, yet again, going to step in and speak with great authority. He says in verses 28–29,

John 7:28–29
28 Then Jesus cried out in the temple, teaching and saying, "You both know Me and know where I am from; and I have not come of Myself, but He who sent Me is true, whom you do not know. 29 I know Him, because I am from Him, and He sent Me."

Jesus first clarified what they did know. The only way He could know what they knew is because He is omniscient. This, again, is God in flesh.

John 7:28
28 Then Jesus cried out in the temple, teaching and saying,

It's the same method we find in John 1:23, when they are asking John the Baptist who he is, and,

John 1:23
23 He said, "I am a voice of one crying in the wilderness, 'Make straight the way of the Lord,' as Isaiah the prophet said."

Jesus is speaking with a loud voice! The Greek word, κράζω means to cry out, to scream, or to shriek. So Jesus is here, teaching in the temple, it says, speaking with passion and vigor, because what He is saying is a

---

[3] Jason Meyer, *Lloyd-Jones on the Christian Life: Doctrine and Life as Fuel and Fire* (Wheaton, IL: Crossway, 2018), 45.

matter of life and death. He preaches aloud, saying, "You both know Me and know where I am from."

John Calvin said that, "There is not a more destructive plague than when men are so intoxicated by the scanty portion of knowledge which they possess, that they boldly reject everything that is contrary to their opinion."[4]

These men are rejecting what they know to be true. They know Christ, as He says, but it is one thing to know about Christ in an informational way, and another thing to know Christ in a transformational way—to know Him personally and in a salvific way.

These men knew Christ. They knew where He was from, as they had already said in John 6:42.

John 6:42
42 "Is not this Jesus, the son of Joseph, whose father and mother we know? How does He now say, 'I have come down out of heaven'?"

So both the Jewish people and the leaders knew Jesus. But Jesus wanted to make something very clear, and that is that they don't know Him for who He truly is. Christ continues to say, in verse 28,

John 7:28
28 "and I have not come of Myself, but He who sent Me is true, whom you do not know."

Jesus is saying, "You know Me, but you don't know My Father, who sent Me to you, that you might have life."

John 1:11
11 He came to His own, and those who were His own did not receive Him.

Have you received Christ? Have you accepted Him? Have you responded to the grace that's been given to you? Because, as it says in John 1:12,

---

[4] John Calvin, *Commentary on the Gospel According to John,* Logos Bible Software, Vol. 1, ed. William Pringle (Bellingham, WA: Faithlife, 2010), 298–99.

John 1:12
12 But as many as received Him, to them He gave the right to become children of God, even to those who believe in His name!

Who do you say that He is? Believe and be saved, for God has given to you the greatest gift, if you will repent and believe the gospel.

They thought they knew God, but Christ knew better. Since they didn't believe in Christ, they certainly didn't believe in God.

In John 14, as we will see, Jesus very clearly says,

John 14:7–11
7 "If you had known Me, you would have known My Father also; from now on you know Him, and have seen Him." 8 Philip said to Him, "Lord, show us the Father, and it is enough for us." 9 Jesus said to him, "Have I been so long with you, and yet you have not come to know Me, Philip? He who has seen Me has seen the Father; how can you say, 'Show us the Father'? 10 Do you not believe that I am in the Father, and the Father is in Me? The words that I say to you I do not speak on My own initiative, but the Father abiding in Me does His works. 11 Believe Me that I am in the Father and the Father is in Me; otherwise believe because of the works themselves."

Jesus says, "You guys don't know Him, the Father, because you know not Me."

So, Christ clarifies, that while these people don't know Him,

John 7:29
29 "I know Him, because I am from Him, and He sent Me."

We see this relationship between God the Father and God the Son. Jesus is saying, "I know Him. He sent Me on a mission to save the lost and redeem the elect."

It's about God. It's all about God. It's all about His glory, and Jesus wants to make this very clear.

These people can do all of these rituals, go to all of the feasts, and they can dress in clothing that makes them look spiritual. They can obtain all of this head knowledge, but what Jesus says is true because He knows

Him. He is here to redeem the lost who will believe. He is here to clarify that these people don't know God, but that they can come to know Him through His Son, whom He has sent—and that is Christ, the Messiah!

So, "Who do you say that I am?"

We have seen the confusion of the people, the clarification of the Teacher, and we see finally, the conviction of the hearers.

THE CONVICTION OF THE HEARERS

The Word of God is certain to do one thing: convict. When conviction comes, there are two options—accept it, or reject it.

Hebrews 4:12
12 For the word of God is living and active and sharper than any two-edged sword, and piercing as far as the division of soul and spirit, of both joints and marrow, and able to judge the thoughts and intentions of the heart.

The Word of God causes penetration, division, and separation, and that is what the words of Christ do here.

After all this crying out, this preaching with passion, this teaching with vigor, the speaking of all that Christ has done, and the conviction of the words of Christ (the Word of God), there is a conflict. Just after Jesus says, in verse 29, "I know Him, because I am from Him, and He sent Me," the passage says,

John 7:30
30 So they were seeking to seize Him; and no man laid his hand on Him, because His hour had not yet come.

The truth caused chaos. The reality of what Christ said caused a desire to seize Him, to kill Him, and to shut Him up. Isn't this what the world wants, to shut Him up? And isn't this what the world has done to so many who claim the seal of Christ?

The problem in our Christian culture is that many of us have been shut up by the world and have been seized. This is the world in which we live. The people of the world want to seize the words of Christ, to take hold of them forcibly, to snatch them away (like the devil), and to grab hold of the grace of God in the lives of people and prevent them from coming to Christ.

John 16:8 reminds us of what conviction does.

John 16:8
8 "And He, when He comes, will convict the world concerning sin and righteousness and judgment;"

While the world will hate this and try to stop it, God is in absolute control, because He is sovereign over the mightiest of men and the craftiest of objectives.

So, we are told that even though they desired to take hold of Christ,

John 7:30
30 no man laid his hand on Him, because His hour had not yet come.

This is God, and there is no man who can stand against the will of God.

The convicting power of Christ's words divided the people. In this convicting question, "Who is Jesus?", we see that they were not yet willing to believe. That is what Christ intended to happen.

But while there was a rejection of Christ, we also see that there was a receptiveness to Christ as well.

John 7:31
31 But many of the crowd believed in Him; and they were saying, "When the Christ comes, He will not perform more signs than those which this man has, will He?"

God is always working. There are some who reject and some who receive. They point out what Jesus says in John 14:11, as a reason for believing, and that is in the power of His works.

John 7:31
31 "When the Christ comes, He will not perform more signs than those which this man has, will He?"

Christ came to seek and to save the lost. All that He does, He does to glorify the Father who sent Him, that you may believe. Believe Him, that

He is in the Father, and that the Father is in Him. Otherwise, He says to, "believe because of the works themselves," (John 14:11).

So this begs the question as we close this chapter, "Who do you say that I am?"

John 20:31
31 these have been written so that you may believe that Jesus is the Christ, the Son of God; and that believing you may have life in His name.

Joshua 24:15
15 "choose for yourselves today whom you will serve…but as for me and my house, we will serve the Lord."

CHAPTER 9

AN INVITATION TO MOVE!
John 7:32–39

The story was told of an extremely cold, winter day. There was a carcass that was floating on the icy Niagara River. An eagle, flying overhead, spied the easy prey below and descended on it. He began to eat. As he did, the water of the river began slowly pushing him toward the falls. Could the eagle not stretch forth his great wings and fly? Could he not, at the very edge of the falls, leap to the safety of the air? Had he not done so a thousand times before? Without worry, he slowly continued to eat. As he ate, the water of the river began moving faster and faster, and closer and closer, to the falls, until the roar of the water began to echo throughout the canyon. The eagle waited until the mists of the falls began rising above his head. Finally, he stretched forth his great wings to fly. Unknown to him, his massive claws had become frozen in the flesh of his prey, and now, attached to the carcass, he was frozen solid and caught in the flow. His fate was sealed. He struggled, and he tried to get away, but he could not, until, at last, the frozen carcass went over the falls and onto the rocks below carrying the eagle along with it. The eagle waited too long.

Don't we tend to reason, like this eagle, that we can hold on just a bit longer? Today, Christ wants to offer you an invitation to move. Don't wait. Don't hold fast to what you have been, but move. This is a message to both believers and unbelievers. It's an invitation to move, before it's too late.

Throughout the Gospel of John and up to this point, Jesus has unmistakably made it clear that He has wanted, desired, preferred, and hoped, that all would respond to this invitation He so regularly provides. This is the invitation to come (John 1:39), the invitation to follow (John 1:43), the invitation to do as He says (John 2:8), the invitation to destroy Him (John 2:19), the invitation to believe (John 3:16); the invitation to drink (John 4:14), the invitation for salvation, the invitation for the kingdom of God, and the invitation to hear, heed, and believe!

There are four things I hope to highlight in this chapter: first, the rejection of the leaders; second, the reaction of the rejected; third, the request of the Christ; and fourth, the results of the responders.

THE REJECTION OF THE LEADERS

A common theme throughout the Book of John is the rejection of the invitations that Christ offers. Jesus, if you recall, is rejected by His own people.

John 1:11
11 He came to His own, and those who were His own did not receive Him.

He was rejected by His own people, Israel, when He claimed to be the Bread of Life. He was the Bread of Life that came down out of heaven, but they did not believe.

John 6:66
66 As a result of this many of His disciples withdrew and were not walking with Him anymore.

Jesus isn't only rejected by His own people and His own disciples, but even worse, He was rejected by His own family. They were preparing to head to Jerusalem for the Feast of Booths, and we are told in John 7:5,

John 7:5
5 For not even His brothers were believing in Him.

And here in our passage, there is no difference. We see the rejection from the Jewish leaders as they turn away from Jesus as Messiah (John 7:1, 19).

The text says,

John 7:32
32 The Pharisees heard the crowd muttering these things about Him, and the chief priests and the Pharisees sent officers to seize Him.

They have had enough. They didn't like Jesus, didn't want to hear another word from Him, and they thought the easiest way to get Jesus gone was to have the temple police seize and kill Him. We see in John 7 that,

John 7:1
1 After these things Jesus was walking in Galilee, for He was unwilling to walk in Judea because the Jews were seeking to kill Him.
And here again in chapter 7, Jesus reminds us that they wanted Him dead.

Jesus also says,

John 7:19
19 "Did not Moses give you the Law, and yet none of you carries out the Law? Why do you seek to kill Me?"

They want Jesus gone. Why? Because Jesus isn't scared to call out sin. He speaks of the wickedness of the heart. He speaks of the hypocrisy of the people. Therefore, they hate Him. They want Him shut up and dead.

So we see in verse 31 that after Jesus spoke, there were some that believed, and here in verse 32, we are reminded that they were talking about it among themselves. It says that,

John 7:32
32 The Pharisees heard the crowd muttering these things about Him

You could say they were whispering. It's what the Greek word (γογγύζω) means, to speak secretly or whisper.[1] They wouldn't even speak up out of fear of the leaders, who were nasty, evil men. In John 20:19, after the death of Christ, Jesus comes to the upper room and meets the disciples there, and the text says,

John 20:19
19 So when it was evening on that day, the first day of the week, and when the doors were shut where the disciples were, for fear of the Jews, Jesus came and stood in their midst and said to them, "Peace be with you."

Also, if you remember from just a few chapters back in John 7:12–13, the text says that,

---

[1] William Arndt, Frederick William Danker, and Walter Bauer, *A Greek-English Lexicon of the New Testament and Other Early Christian literature*, 3rd ed. (Chicago: University of Chicago Press, 2001), 204.

John 7:12–13
12 There was much grumbling among the crowds concerning Him; some were saying, "He is a good man"; others were saying, "No, on the contrary, He leads the people astray." 13 Yet no one was speaking openly of Him for fear of the Jews.

Or when the blind boy received his sight,

John 9:18–22
18 The Jews then did not believe it of him, that he had been blind and had received sight, until they called the parents of the very one who had received his sight, 19 and questioned them, saying, "Is this your son, who you say was born blind? Then how does he now see?" 20 His parents answered them and said, "We know that this is our son, and that he was born blind; 21 but how he now sees, we do not know; or who opened his eyes, we do not know. Ask him; he is of age, he will speak for himself." 22 His parents said this because they were afraid of the Jews; for the Jews had already agreed that if anyone confessed Him to be Christ, he was to be put out of the synagogue.

These leaders inspired fear in the people, but they couldn't scare Jesus. He called them for what they were, like in Matthew 23:27,

Matthew 23:27
27 "Woe to you, scribes and Pharisees, hypocrites! For you are like whitewashed tombs which on the outside appear beautiful, but inside they are full of dead men's bones and all uncleanness."

They rejected Him. They sought His life, and they will continue to do so over the next six months until they have our Lord crucified. So when we come to John 7:33, we see,

John 7:33
33 Therefore Jesus said, "For a little while longer I am with you, then I go to Him who sent Me."

Jesus is saying, "My time here is short, and because you have rejected me as Lord, when I go to Him who sent Me (God the Father), I will no longer be available!"

And because of this, because of their rejection, He now gives us some of the most terrible news. It is in verse 34 that we see the rejection from Jesus, after the Jewish leaders have first rejected Him. He says,

John 7:34
34 "You will seek Me, and will not find Me; and where I am, you cannot come."

Jesus is saying, "You will look for Me. You will search for Me. You will hunt for Me. But you will be found lacking."

It's a statement of fact. It's the same cry from Proverbs 1:27–28,

Proverbs 1:27–28
27 When your dread comes like a storm And your calamity comes like a whirlwind, When distress and anguish come upon you. 28 "Then they will call on me, but I will not answer; They will seek me diligently but they will not find me,"

They will seek Him.

Philippians 2:9–11
8 Being found in appearance as a man, He humbled Himself by becoming obedient to the point of death, even death on a cross. 9 For this reason also, God highly exalted Him, and bestowed on Him the name which is above every name, 10 so that at the name of Jesus EVERY KNEE WILL BOW, of those who are in heaven and on earth and under the earth, 11 and that every tongue will confess that Jesus Christ is Lord, to the glory of God the Father.

They rejected the Christ, and now, the Christ has rejected them. Heaven's doors have just been closed on these people.

Romans 1:28
28 And just as they did not see fit to acknowledge God any longer, God gave them over to a depraved mind, to do those things which are not proper,

They have rejected Him, and Christ says in John 7:34,

John 7:34
34 "You will seek Me, and will not find Me; and where I am, you cannot come."

Have you considered that your opportunity to respond to the gospel may come to a close? Don't wait too long, because sooner or later it will be too late to let go of the things of this world. He is coming here, or you are going there. As I heard Paul Washer once say, "I've got good news, and I've got bad news. The good news is that Jesus is here. The bad news is that Jesus is here. It just depends on which side of the line you are on!"

The invitation is to move, come, and receive Christ as Lord. So we can clearly see the rejection of the leaders, and now we turn to the reaction of the rejected.

THE REACTION OF THE REJECTED

They are confused. They have been confused, but now they don't understand where Jesus is going. They are focused on the physical, not the spiritual.

John 7:35
35 The Jews then said to one another, "Where does this man intend to go that we will not find Him?"

If Jesus is just a man, they would be able to find Him. But we know that He is more than a man. He is God in flesh. So they try to come to grips with where He might go, and verse 35 continues with them saying,

John 7:35
35 "He is not intending to go to the dispersion among the Greeks, and teach the Greeks, is He?"

The Jews were the chosen ones. We know that from the Abrahamic Covenants found in Genesis 12; 13; 15; 17; and 22:17. Scripture also says,

Deuteronomy 14:2
2 "For you are a holy people to the LORD your God, and the LORD has chosen you to be a people for His own possession out of all the peoples who are on the face of the earth."

Here in the New Testament, we see the same idea,

Romans 3:2
2 First of all, that they were entrusted with the oracles of God.
Jesus even stated that they were special, and that He had a special
purpose for coming.

And again,

Matthew 15:24
24 But He answered and said, "I was sent only to the lost sheep of the
house of Israel."

So going to the Greeks would have been wrong to these leaders. And
because of their rejection, we will see in Romans 3:29,

Romans 3:29
29 Or is God the God of Jews only? Is He not the God of Gentiles also?
Yes, of Gentiles also,

The Greeks wouldn't miss out on the opportunity because God has a
larger purpose, for not only the Jews, but the Gentiles. So the leaders are
confused, and their problem is that they are more concerned about who
won't get in than about themselves getting in.

How about you? Do you find yourself more worried about others getting
into heaven than yourself? That is what these men are doing. These men
have been shut out of heaven, and yet they're worried about the Gentiles
getting the gospel. Their response is one of sheer confusion when they
ask,

John 7:36
**36 "What is this statement that He said, 'You will seek Me, and will not
find Me; and where I am, you cannot come'?"**

The people are spiritually blind and unable to see, so they are confused.
They misunderstand, and they have no clue. And they have missed it
because they are spiritually dead.

John 3:20

20 "For everyone who does evil hates the Light, and does not come to the Light for fear that his deeds will be exposed."

They are dead. They are blind. They cannot see the things of God.

Romans 8:6–8
6 For the mind set on the flesh is death, but the mind set on the Spirit is life and peace, 7 because the mind set on the flesh is hostile toward God; for it does not subject itself to the law of God, for it is not even able to do so, 8 and those who are in the flesh cannot please God.

This was us. Many have changed, but it is easy to still find oneself living in the flesh. This does not please God, and He will not tarry forever. The stage is set, the work is done, and soon He will burst through the clouds—and everything that has ever been made will fall on its face in worship.

At that point, for those who have rejected Him, it will be too late.

Jesus sees the great need. He sees the great rejection, but He also sees the desperate situation of the crowd. There were so many people nearby at this feast who couldn't understand; and Jesus doesn't skip a beat.

THE REQUEST OF CHRIST

The great invitation is now given. This is a special and powerful illustration that Christ is about to provide. The text reads,

John 7:37
37 Now on the last day, the great day of the feast, Jesus stood and cried out, saying, "If anyone is thirsty, let him come to Me and drink."

It's the last day of the Feast of Booths, and they have been celebrating for a whole week. The great day has now come, and they will continue to do what they have done.

It was a daily ritual that took place: "The people would, each morning, gather at the temple and they would come with an etrog (citrus fruit) in their left hand and a lulab in their right hand. This was a combination of three different branches (palms, willow, and myrtle), and once everyone was ready and gathered, the priest would hold out a golden pitcher and head towards the pool of Siloam. The people would wave their lulabs in rhythm and sing different psalms, and when they approached the pool of Siloam, the priest would dip the golden pitcher and gather water, while the people would recite some beautiful words from Isaiah 12:3.

Isaiah 12:3
3 Therefore you will joyously draw water From the springs of salvation.

The crowds would march back to the temple, going through the Water Gate with trumpets blasting. They would circle the altar and pour out the water. This was a daily event. But on the last day, they circled it seven times, as a reminder of the victory in Jericho which ended the wilderness wandering. And after this, they would pour out the water."[2]

It's here where we see Jesus cry out,

John 7:37
37 Jesus stood and cried out, saying, "If anyone is thirsty, let him come to Me and drink."

This term, "cried out," again, is a term that means to cry out loudly with passion, and with a voice of urgency. With this volume, passion, and urgency, He says, "If anyone is thirsty, let him come to Me and drink."

He is the One who offers living water—the same water offered to the woman at the well.

John 4:13–14
13 Jesus answered and said to her, "Everyone who drinks of this water will thirst again; 14 but whoever drinks of the water that I will give him shall never thirst; but the water that I will give him will become in him a well of water springing up to eternal life."

Christ is calling you today. He is inviting you to come and move toward Him when He says, "If anyone is thirsty, let him come to Me and drink." Stop chasing after things that cannot give you more than temporal satisfaction. "Come to Me and drink [from Me]," He says.

---

[2] R. Kent Hughes, *John: That You May Believe*, Preaching the Word (Wheaton, IL: Crossway, 2014), 216.

Notice what's happening in this invitation. First, consider the invitation's extent. He says, "If anyone is thirsty, let him come to Me and drink." Anyone. This invitation for all is also seen in Matthew 11:28,

Matthew 11:28
"Come to Me, all who are weary and heavy-laden, and I will give you rest."

In 2 Peter 3:9, we see that the Lord doesn't want any to perish,

2 Peter 3:9
9 The Lord is not slow about His promise, as some count slowness, but is patient toward you, not wishing for any to perish but for all to come to repentance.

In 1 Timothy 2:3–4, we see that God wants all people to be saved,

1 Timothy 2:3–4
3 This is good and acceptable in the sight of God our Savior, 4 who desires all men to be saved and to come to the knowledge of the truth.

Romans 10:13
13 "WHOEVER WILL CALL ON THE NAME OF THE LORD WILL BE SAVED."

Notice the three verbs that drive home this passage in John 7, especially verse 37. They are the verbs, "thirst," "come," and "drink."

"Thirst" means to hunger, to desire, and to want something greatly. If you are reading this today, and you have a thirst and longing for deliverance, hope, peace, forgiveness, and salvation, He says, "Drink!" If you are reading this today, and you say, "I have a desire to be delivered from the power of sin," He says, "Drink!"

"Come" means to move toward, and respond in trust to, the grace that's been given. Jesus says, in Luke 9:23, "If anyone wishes to come after Me." To come. Take action.

"Drink" means to receive, take hold of, obtain, ingest, and accept. It was what Jesus told the woman at the well in John 4:13–14. Unless you drink, you will die.

Jesus speaks this truth in John 7:37, in connection with the festival's activity of pouring.

John 7:37
37 "If anyone is thirsty, let him come to Me and drink."

Do not go to the things of this world. Do not go to the temporal things of this life. "We have become satisfied with mere church, mere religious exertion, mere numbers and buildings—the things we can do. There is nothing wrong with these things, but they are no more than foam left by the surf on the ocean of God's glory and goodness."[3]

We see, the rejection of the leader, the reaction of the rejected, the request of Christ, and finally, see the results of the responders.

THE RESULTS OF THE RESPONDERS

What would be the results for those who did come and drink?

John 7:38–39
38 "He who believes in Me, as the Scripture said, 'From his innermost being will flow rivers of living water.'" 39 But this He spoke of the Spirit, whom those who believed in Him were to receive; for the Spirit was not yet given, because Jesus was not yet glorified.

When you thirst for forgiveness, when you seek grace and mercy and you come, you respond to the working of the Holy Spirit. When you trust, you partake of the Living Water.

Now, you receive the Holy Spirit at conversion. This was not the case in their day, because Jesus hadn't yet been glorified. This doesn't mean the Holy Spirit wasn't working. But Christ said,

John 14:16
16 "I will ask the Father, and He will give you another Helper, that He may be with you forever;"

But when you are truly saved, Jesus says, in verse 38,

---

[3] Ben Patterson, *Deepening Your Conversation with God*, (Bloomington, MN: Bethany House, 2001), 171).

John 7:38–39
38 "He who believes in Me, as the Scripture said, 'From his innermost being will flow rivers of living water.'"

You will be doers of the Word. You will be sharers of your faith. You will be promoters of the gospel. You will be agents for the King of Kings and for the Lord of Lords. You will be Spirit-filled, like a flowing river, for others to see.

It's an invitation to move into a personal relationship with Jesus Christ, in whom you trust by faith alone for salvation.

Your invitation is here. All who are thirsty, come and drink from Him, and He will give you life, and life abundantly.

CHAPTER 10

WILL YOU CHOOSE TO BELIEVE CHRIST?
John 7:40–52

I heard a story once of a farmer who hired a man to work for him around his property. The first task he gave him was to paint the shed. The farmer thought that task should take about three days for the man to complete. But to the farmer's surprise, the hired man finished all the work in one day. The farmer then set him up to cut some wood, thinking that task would require about four days. The hired man finished in a day and a half, to the farmer's amazement. The next task was to sort out a large pile of potatoes. The hired man was to arrange them into three piles: seed potatoes, food for the hogs, and potatoes that were good enough to sell. The farmer said it was a small job, and it shouldn't take long at all for the hired man. At the end of the day, the farmer came back and found the hired man had barely started. "What's the matter here?" the farmer asked. "I can work hard, but I can't make decisions." replied the hired man.

Making decisions can be a hard thing to accomplish. Decisions can be choices that twist us up and hold us down. Making decisions can simply paralyze us. But we must all make choices in this life. And this section of John is all about making decisions—about whom you choose to believe, and how you respond to the truth of Christ.

Jesus was there on the last day of the Feast of Booths. At this feast, they were celebrating God's provision when the people of God wandered in the wilderness for forty years. On the last day of the festival, the people would circle the altar seven times, and then pour out the water. At that moment, Jesus calls out with a loud voice,

John 7:37–38
37 "If anyone is thirsty, let him come to Me and drink. 38 He who believes in Me, as the Scripture said, 'From his innermost being will flow rivers of living water.'"

The impact was huge. It was the greatest invitation in history. But that invitation created an opportunity for choosing. That is the context as we consider this text.

There are three things in this passage that will affect the choices you make. First, we see a division among the people; second, we see a delusion among the people; and finally, we see a devotion among the people.

A DIVISION AMONG THE PEOPLE

This portion of Scripture follows after Jesus' invitation. Once Jesus made that claim and gave that invitation, the people were left with a choice. They could either choose to believe Christ, or they could choose to reject Christ. What was true then is also true today.

There are no other options. God didn't leave room for error here. Christ died, and His blood paid for all; you either choose to accept Him, or you choose to reject Him.

Here was the dilemma among the people. The text reads,

John 7:40–43
40 Some of the people therefore, when they heard these words, were saying, "This certainly is the Prophet." 41 Others were saying, "This is the Christ." Still others were saying, "Surely the Christ is not going to come from Galilee, is He? 42 Has not the Scripture said that the Christ comes from the descendants of David, and from Bethlehem, the village where David was?" 43 So a division occurred in the crowd because of Him. 44 Some of them wanted to seize Him, but no one laid hands on Him.

The division was caused because of the people's confidence.

John 7:40–41
40 Some of the people therefore, when they heard these words, were saying, "This certainly is the Prophet." 41 Others were saying, "This is the Christ."

These are the ones who believe, choose Christ, and come to the invitation that He has just offered up. The people rightfully respond that this is, "the Prophet."

Deuteronomy 18:15–18
15 "The LORD your God will raise up for you a prophet like me from among you, from your countrymen, you shall listen to him. 16 This is

according to all that you asked of the LORD your God in Horeb on the day of the assembly, saying, 'Let me not hear again the voice of the LORD my God, let me not see this great fire anymore, or I will die.' 17 The LORD said to me, 'They have spoken well. 18 I will raise up a prophet from among their countrymen like you, and I will put My words in his mouth, and he shall speak to them all that I command him.'"

These people understand who this is. This is the Messiah, the great Prophet. They are confident.

When we come to the New Testament, Peter and Stephen promote this same idea.

Look at Peter's sermon about the Prophet, Christ, in Acts 3:22–23,

Acts 3:22–23
22 "Moses said, 'THE LORD GOD WILL RAISE UP FOR YOU A PROPHET LIKE ME FROM YOUR BRETHREN; TO HIM YOU SHALL GIVE HEED to everything He says to you. 23 And it will be that every soul that does not heed that prophet shall be utterly destroyed from among the people.'"

Stephen, in Acts 7:37, points out this same idea when He is stoned for his preaching. He calls these people "stiff-necked" (Acts 7:51).

John 7:40–41
40 "This certainly is the Prophet." 41 Others were saying, "This is the Christ."

There was new boldness in their lungs. They have chosen and voiced it, which is so different from what they were doing.

Recall John 7:13, 32, and 41. There is no more whispering. There is a new boldness. They had believed. They had come thirsty, and they had drunk from the Living Water.

The division happens from having confidence in Christ, or from living confused, like many of these people were.

In John 7:41–42, we find another group.

John 7:41b–42
41b Still others were saying, "Surely the Christ is not going to come from Galilee, is He? 42 Has not the Scripture said that the Christ comes from the descendants of David, and from Bethlehem, the village where David was?"

There was mass confusion among the people. Their first problem is a confusion about where Christ is from. "Surely the Christ is not going to come from Galilee, is He?" This is a trivial confusion, yet one that causes the people to reject Christ and causes division.

We know that Christ was from Bethlehem. Their division and rejection is due to a lack of investigation.

Matthew 2:1–2
1 Now after Jesus was born in Bethlehem of Judea in the days of Herod the king, magi from the east arrived in Jerusalem, saying, 2 "Where is He who has been born King of the Jews? For we saw His star in the east and have come to worship Him."

These people are confused. They're mad, out of their minds, and causing division because of their confusion. There's no telling how many they are leading astray out of their lack of understanding.

Luke 2:4–7
4 Joseph also went up from Galilee, from the city of Nazareth, to Judea, to the city of David which is called Bethlehem, because he was of the house and family of David, 5 in order to register along with Mary, who was engaged to him, and was with child. 6 While they were there, the days were completed for her to give birth. 7 And she gave birth to her firstborn son; and she wrapped Him in cloths, and laid Him in a manger, because there was no room for them in the inn.

How about verse 11 of the same chapter?

Luke 2:11
11 "for today in the city of David there has been born for you a Savior, who is Christ the Lord."

How about verse 15?

Luke 2:15
15 When the angels had gone away from them into heaven, the shepherds
began saying to one another, "Let us go straight to Bethlehem then, and
see this thing that has happened which the Lord has made known to us."

They reject Christ, and they cause division out of mass confusion.

Jesus was from Bethlehem. He did meet the qualifications, and they
would have seen this if they had simply looked. They failed to
investigate.

Don't stand on confusion. Don't reject Jesus because of laziness like
these people did. Seek for yourself. Read the Word of God, listen to the
preaching of His Word, and respond to the Holy Spirit when He calls
you. Choose to believe Christ.

Because of the contrast between some people's confidence and others'
confusion, division arose.

John 7:43
43 So a division occurred in the crowd because of Him.

Notice that Jesus hasn't said a word. They are fighting over who He is,
and they are all making a choice in trying to understand. Will you choose
to believe in Christ or man?

Their division caused a response, because the leaders and those who
failed to believe wanted Him dead.

John 7:44
44 Some of them wanted to seize Him, but no one laid hands on Him.

Either you are for Him, or you are against Him.

Matthew 12:30
30 "He who is not with Me is against Me; and he who does not gather
with Me scatters."

There is no middle ground with the gospel. Don't allow the division from
people's confusion to distract you from choosing Christ.

A DELUSION AMONG THE PEOPLE

No matter the evidence, these leaders will not believe. Unless God by His grace reveals Himself, the Scripture says that people are not even able to come.

John 6:44
44 "No one can come to Me unless the Father who sent Me draws him; and I will raise him up on the last day."

That is why when you feel the Lord leading you to believe, you must respond. Forget what was, and forget what might be. Respond in the now.

John 6:40
40 "For this is the will of My Father, that everyone who beholds the Son and believes in Him will have eternal life, and I Myself will raise him up on the last day."

Not these people here, though. Their unbelief caused their own delusion. We are told that,

John 7:45–49
45 The officers then came to the chief priests and Pharisees, and they said to them, "Why did you not bring Him?" 46 The officers answered, "Never has a man spoken the way this man speaks." 47 The Pharisees then answered them, "You have not also been led astray, have you? 48 No one of the rulers or Pharisees has believed in Him, has he? 49 But this crowd which does not know the Law is accursed."

The people are disillusioned in that they believe the officers, or the "temple police," are deceived.

These are the ones who have just had Heaven's door shut in their face, and they are claiming those who believe are the ones who are deceived. They are disillusioned.

John 7:45
45 The officers then came to the chief priests and Pharisees, and they said to them, "Why did you not bring Him?"

They had been asked in John 7:32 to go seize Him, but when they go to do the job, they are amazed.

These are religious men, not Romans who would have done as they were told and seized Him. But these officers wanted to know why He wasn't brought back, because, as the officers said,

John 7:46
46 The officers answered, "Never has a man spoken the way this man speaks."

In verse 47, we see the Pharisees' response,

John 7:47
47 The Pharisees then answered them, "You have not also been led astray, have you?"

They are deceived and disillusioned. They are dead men walking. They are tricked into thinking that they are right and that God in flesh is wrong. In reality, they are the ones who are astray.

It's no different today.

The church, the town, the county, the state, the nation, and the world is full of those who are astray. They are tricked and deceived by the enemy to think they have done enough good to get to Heaven. See what Scripture says in Proverbs 14:12.

Proverbs 14:12
12 There is a way which seems right to a man, But its end is the way of death.

There are many people walking around under the illusion that they are saved. Their problem is the same problem of these people: they have not believed in Christ. They have not responded to the gospel. They think that because they do certain things, they will make it in. However, that's not the way that God works.

God says that he who wants to come first must come last. He says that the one who wants to live must die. He says that unless one first acknowledges that he or she has sinned against a holy and righteous God, that person is not saved. You may have lived a good life, but you haven't lived a perfect life, and neither has anyone else.

Your sin has made a separation between you and your God. Remember that sin is anything you think, say, or do, that breaks God's law.

Have you ever stolen anything? Have you ever told a lie? Ever looked at a man or woman in lust? If so, then you have sinned, and the Bible says that the wages of that sin is death (Rom 6:23).

You can't love God enough to get you into heaven, but God has loved you enough to make a way for you in which you can be forgiven, and that is through His Son, Jesus Christ (the One whom these men reject).

Matthew 7:22–23
22 "Many will say to Me on that day, 'Lord, Lord, did we not prophesy in Your name, and in Your name cast out demons, and in Your name perform many miracles?' 23 And then I will declare to them, 'I never knew you; DEPART FROM ME, YOU WHO PRACTICE LAWLESSNESS.'"

The text says,

John 7:48
48 "No one of the rulers or Pharisees has believed in Him, has he?"

Those who have been led astray never want to be alone. Evil loves company. Remember Adam and Eve; that moment in history has ongoing results. She gave the fruit to him, and the principle that evil loves company was born.

For them to say, "No one of the rulers or Pharisees has believed in Him, has he?" what they are saying is: "If He was the Messiah, we would know, and we would believe. But He isn't, so we aren't believing, and none of the others are either. You are alone in your belief."

But that, too, is false.

John 12:42–43
42 Nevertheless many even of the rulers believed in Him, but because of the Pharisees they were not confessing Him, for fear that they would be put out of the synagogue; 43 for they loved the approval of men rather than the approval of God.

They weren't alone. It's yet another false statement. The text continues,

John 7:48–49
**48 "No one of the rulers or Pharisees has believed in Him, has he? 49
But this crowd which does not know the Law is accursed."**

They're saying that because these people are uneducated, or untrained, or haven't been through the religious system, they are therefore accursed.

God has shut the door on these people, and they are casting their judgement against those who believe. They are so blind to their sin.

In John 7, they are essentially saying, "We have the knowledge of the Torah (the Law). We would be the first to know if this was the Messiah, but not these accursed, untrained people."

Many in their unbelief will say that there is no God, but it says,

Psalm 14:1
*1 The fool has said in his heart, "There is no God." They are corrupt,
they have committed abominable deeds; There is no one who does good.*

And when we come to Romans, the text reads,

Romans 1:18–22
*18 For the wrath of God is revealed from heaven against all ungodliness
and unrighteousness of men who suppress the truth in unrighteousness,
19 because that which is known about God is evident within them; for
God made it evident to them. 20 For since the creation of the world His
invisible attributes, His eternal power and divine nature, have been
clearly seen, being understood through what has been made, so that they
are without excuse. 21 For even though they knew God, they did not
honor Him as God or give thanks, but they became futile in their
speculations, and their foolish heart was darkened. 22 Professing to be
wise, they became fools,*

Will you believe Christ or reject Him?

A DEVOTION AMONG THE PEOPLE

It's a two-fold devotion. There is a brave one who stands and speaks up.

John 7:50–52
50 Nicodemus (he who came to Him before, being one of them) said to them, 51 "Our Law does not judge a man unless it first hears from him and knows what he is doing, does it?" 52 They answered him, "You are not also from Galilee, are you? Search, and see that no prophet arises out of Galilee."

Not all of the religious leaders have rejected. Nicodemus has taken a stand here. He has already visited Christ in the private of the night, but now he has come publicly in reminding his colleagues of the Law. He is being honest.

John 7:51
51 "Our Law does not judge a man unless it first hears from him and knows what he is doing, does it?"

He takes a stand on honesty, but they have dug in. They are devoted to hostility. They have caused division, they have lived out of delusion, and they have hearts full of hate, rage, and disbelief. Nothing can stop them from rejecting Jesus.

But Nicodemus takes a stand for Jesus in saying He deserves a fair trial, and he is mocked by them.

John 7:52
52 "You are not also from Galilee, are you?"

Essentially, they're saying, "You're not worthless, too, are you, Nicodemus?" They are full of pride and arrogance, and they would, at any cost, continue to reject and distract others from believing.

The words of Nicodemus are truth, and the truth penetrates their souls. And so, they continue to show their ignorance, and they challenge him.

John 7:52
52 "Search, and see that no prophet arises out of Galilee."

They know it all. Ironically, they are mocking Nicodemus for speaking truth, and they are so mad that they are not even thinking straight.

Don't stand for hostility. Stand rather, like Nicodemus, for honesty. Don't reject the gospel because you're living in confusion, or because you're devoted to hostility. You have lots of choices to make in life, just like Nicodemus. While we don't see it unfold here, Nicodemus was there in the darkest hours of Christ's life. He made the decision to follow Christ.

When you're willing to defend your faith, persecution will follow. Nicodemus made the decision to stand with Christ, no matter the cost.

You, too, have a choice today. Will you choose to believe Christ? Or will you choose to reject Him?

CHAPTER 11

THE GRACE OF JESUS
John 7:53–8:11

Grace. It's a key term that impacts all of humanity. Grace is a gift, that, by God's doing, is given to man, in spite of us not deserving it. It is because of God that we receive all the benefits that Christ has purchased. It's this grace that He has lavished upon us.

It was John Stott who said, "Grace is God loving, God stopping, God coming to the rescue, God giving himself generously in and through Jesus Christ."[1]

The writer of Hebrews says,

Hebrews 13:9
9 for it is good for the heart to be strengthened by grace,

Grace is something we all need. Grace is something that only God can give, and we should (and need to) search for it as a treasure of greatest value.

Grace is needed. It's how we are saved, for the Scripture says,

Ephesians 2:4–5
4 But God, being rich in mercy, because of His great love with which He loved us, 5 even when we were dead in our transgressions, made us alive together with Christ (by grace you have been saved,

Grace is key, but grace wasn't free. Rather, grace cost Christ everything!

- *We see the grace of God begin in the Garden of Eden when God killed an animal to cover the sin of Adam and Eve (Gen 3:21).*

- *We see the grace of God when God delivered His people out of Israel, and they walked through on dry land (Exod 14:30).*

---

[1] Max Lucado, *Grace: More Than We Deserve, Greater Than We Imagine* (Nashville: Thomas Nelson, 2014), 15.

- *We see the grace of God in Rahab the prostitute as God spared her life and the others with her (Josh 6:25).*

- *We see the grace of God in how He provided a great fish to come and swallow up Jonah, who was running in rebellion from God (Jonah 1:17).*

- *In the New Testament, we are told that we are called out by God through grace (Gal 1:15–16).*

- *We believe in Jesus Christ through grace (Acts 18:27).*

We are told in Romans 3:23–24 that we are justified by grace.

Romans 3:23–24
23 for all have sinned and fall short of the glory of God, 24 being justified as a gift by His grace through the redemption which is in Christ Jesus;

Grace upon grace. It's key to the foundations of faith, and it's key in this passage of John. We are going to see the extraordinary grace of our Lord Jesus.

No doubt there is much debate about this portion of Scripture. The debate is that this portion of Scripture isn't found in the earlier manuscripts. This has even caused some to question the integrity of the text. But nothing we find in John 7:53–8:11 is contradictory with the rest of Scripture. What we find, I believe, is an event that has really taken place and portrays a great and valuable, theologically sound scene in John's narrative.

These passages are found in the later manuscripts, and because we can't be fully certain they were added later, we preach them. It's not directly or indirectly at odds with the Scripture we hold in the highest regards. So "we hold to this pericope without loss of rights or privileges which has stood the test of time for over 1,300 years."[2]

As we embark on John 8, we come face to face with grace.

---

[2] Edward Klink III, *John*, Zondervan Exegetical Commentary on the New Testament, ed. Clinton E. Arnold (Grand Rapids: Zondervan, 2016), 390.

There are four things in this passage that will drive home the reality of grace: first, we must be committed Christians; second, we must be discerning Christians; third, we must be compelling Christians; and finally , we must be compassionate Christians.

WE MUST BE COMMITTED CHRISTIANS

Whatever Christ was committed to, we also must be committed to as Christians.

Our commitment as Christians should bring about humility. When the leaders were mocking Nicodemus, they said,

John 7:52
52 "You are not also from Galilee, are you? Search, and see that no prophet arises out of Galilee."

And the text says,

John 7:53–8:1
53 Everyone went to his home. 1 But Jesus went to the Mount of Olives.

The text says something very simple and vague, but something stands out, and that is that everyone went to his home, but Jesus went to the Mount of Olives. Jesus was committed to humility.

This recalls the words of Jesus in Matthew,

Matthew 8:20
20 Jesus said to him, "The foxes have holes and the birds of the air have nests, but the Son of Man has nowhere to lay His head."

While everyone went home, Jesus went to the Mount of Olives. It's a humbling thought. Not only did Christ not have a place to call home, but God in flesh was born into this world in a stable, because Luke 2:7 says that there was no room in the inn.

Christ is not chasing after the things of this world. Rather, He is on task. Jesus could have had anything He wanted, but He was committed to humility.

Are you committed to humility, or is your life built on pride?

Jesus was not only fully committed to humility, but He was committed to persistence.

John 8:2
2 Early in the morning He came again into the temple, and all the people were coming to Him; and He sat down and began to teach them.

The people have gone their way home. Jesus went to camp out at the Mount of Olives, which is just across the Kidron valley.

Regardless, the text says, "Early in the morning He came again into the temple." Yet we keep hearing that no one laid hands on Him. And now, after just one night's rest, He comes again to that place where He knows He is going to be mocked. But Jesus is persistent.

How many of us today have laid down or are just going through the motions in regards to our faith? Jesus has not. He is dedicated to the work which the Father has given Him to do. He is faithful. He is unwavering. He is motivated by a bigger purpose. He is diligent, passionate, and on-task.

Everyone else is just floating on the river, headed downstream, and Jesus is going the other way. He is swimming upstream.

We must be committed Christians, because, if we are going to portray the grace of God, if you and I are going to be like Christ, then we must start living like Christ.

Galatians 2:20
20 I have been crucified with Christ; and it is no longer I who live, but Christ lives in me; and the life which I now live in the flesh I live by faith in the Son of God, who loved me and gave Himself up for me.

Christ was committed to what the Father had called Him to do.

John 8:2
2 Early in the morning He came again into the temple, and all the people were coming to Him; and He sat down and began to teach them.

Are you committed? Maybe you're living in your own strength and not in His. Maybe you're chasing after everything else but that which is eternal. You're tired, you're hurting, and you're lonely, because you're not living for Jesus.

Jesus was committed because He was on task. Are you headed upstream with a purpose, or are you floating downstream with the rest of the world?

I went to dinner with some friends some time ago, and we talked about this very idea. They asked their kids, "Why not just stop swimming? Why not just jump on the float like everyone else and enjoy the nice things of life? Why not float with the current of the culture?" One of the kids said, "Because there is a waterfall at the end, and I simply choose not to believe that." She was right.

WE MUST BE DISCERNING CHRISTIANS

As Christians, we must master the ability to judge well.

Not everyone that says, "Lord, Lord," will enter the kingdom of God (Matt 7:21), and not everyone that says he has your best interest in mind means it. We have to do better at being discerning Christians.

"Discernment simply means judgment and refers to the ability to adequately determine whether something is good or bad, healthy or unhealthy, necessary or unnecessary, desirable or undesirable; or within our own Christian point of view, evil or godly."[3]

Jesus gives us a great example here in our text.

John 8:3–6
3 The scribes and the Pharisees brought a woman caught in adultery, and having set her in the center of the court, 4 they said to Him, "Teacher, this woman has been caught in adultery, in the very act. 5 Now in the Law Moses commanded us to stone such women; what then do You say?" 6 They were saying this, testing Him, so that they might

[3] Brent L. Bolin, "Problems in the Church, Part 2: A Lack of Discernment in Believers / The Church, *Faith Bible Ministries—An Online Study of the Bible*, September 22, 2017, accessed March 24, 2023, https://faithbibleministriesblog.com/2017/09/22/problems-in-the-church-part-2-a-lack-of-discernment-in-believers-the-church-3/.

have grounds for accusing Him. But Jesus stooped down and with His finger wrote on the ground.

The scribes and the Pharisees, while they are found together in the other Gospels, are not found together anywhere else in the Gospel of John. It's one of the debates as to why this portion is inserted into the Book of John at a later date. Regardless, these scribes (or, you could say, experts of the Law, or lawyers) were found together commonly with the Pharisees. The Pharisees were keen on the oral traditions.

These two groups come together and approach Jesus. They have a plan in place, but even without the text saying so, someone with discernment would grasp that they really care nothing about getting answers from Jesus. Jesus' discernment transcends even this, because He knows the intentions of these people.

These men have one purpose, and that is to accuse Jesus. There is nothing left out here.

The scribes and the Pharisees say,

John 8:4–5
4 "Teacher, this woman has been caught in adultery, in the very act. 5 Now in the Law Moses commanded us to stone such women; what then do You say?"

Jesus is very discerning as to their objective, but He focuses less on their wrong motives, and more on their misuse of Scripture. We must discern the truth of God's Word.

John 8:5
5 "Now in the Law, Moses commanded us to stone such women;"

Is this indeed what the Law says? The Law was to be followed perfectly. So, is this right perfectly? It doesn't seem so.

Look at Exodus 20:14.

Exodus 20:14
14 "You shall not commit adultery."

That's wrong. It's sinful and against God's standard. No one negates that. But stoning her? Let's look at where they come up with this from.

Leviticus 20:10
10 "If there is a man who commits adultery with another man's wife, one who commits adultery with his friend's wife, the adulterer and the adulteress shall surely be put to death."

So there, the Law says that this woman could die, but again, the Law requires us to break it and fulfill it perfectly.

Where is the man? Look at Deuteronomy 22:23–24.

Deuteronomy 22:23–24
23 "If there is a girl who is a virgin engaged to a man, and another man finds her in the city and lies with her, 24 then you shall bring them both out to the gate of that city and you shall stone them to death; the girl, because she did not cry out in the city, and the man, because he has violated his neighbor's wife. Thus you shall purge the evil from among you."

They are trying to trap Him on Jewish Law. There is but one answer, and that is to stone her as the Law requires. But they're flawed, "because according to biblical law in such cases both the man and the women who had committed adultery should have been stoned."[4]

Look closely at the text. They said,

John 8:4
4 they said to Him, "Teacher, this woman has been caught in adultery, in the very act.

Where is the man? The man and the woman should be sitting here in this court. But listen. The scribes and the Pharisees care nothing about this sin. They care nothing about the man and what he did, and they probably care nothing about what this woman did. They simply wanted to use her as a pawn. In addition, Jesus isn't a judge. At best they call him, "Rabbi," or "Teacher". It's all a show.

---

[4] J. Ramsey Michaels, *The Gospel of John*, The New International Commentary on the New Testament (Grand Rapids, MI: Eerdmans, 2010), 496.

John 8:6
6 They were saying this, testing Him, so that they might have grounds for accusing Him. But Jesus stooped down and with His finger wrote on the ground.

He didn't acknowledge the error before Him. Jesus had discerned the truth of His Word. He had seen their plan, which had raised the reality of just how holy God is. The Law brings forth wrath.

Romans 4:15
15 for the Law brings about wrath, but where there is no law, there also is no violation.

Romans 2:12
12 For all who have sinned without the Law will also perish without the Law, and all who have sinned under the Law will be judged by the Law;

How can God forgive sinners? How can Jesus not stone this woman? She has broken the very Law of God! I'll tell you how. "The sacrificial work of Jesus Christ satisfied the demands of God's justice."[5]

Remember, Jesus is on task, and He is absolutely discerning.

We, too, must be more discerning of the Word. When we know the Word, we will be able to discern the hearts of wicked men, more like Jesus.

Jeremiah 17:9
"The heart is more deceitful than all else And is desperately sick; Who can understand it?"

It's a must.

WE MUST BE COMPELLING CHRISTIANS

When something is compelling, it drives action. To be compelling is to be truthful. The truth of God's Word is compelling; it's convicting.

---

[5] John MacArthur, *John 1–11*, MacArthur New Testament Commentary, Vol. 11 (Chicago: Moody Publishers, 2006), 16.

John 8:6
6 They were saying this, testing Him, so that they might have grounds for accusing Him. But Jesus stooped down and with His finger wrote on the ground.

We are not sure what He wrote. "But the Greek word here used, means to write against!"[6] Some say that He was writing the sins of the accusers here in the sand. It's pure speculation, but it would make perfect sense.

As He is writing, the text says that they kept nagging. It says,

John 8:7
7 But when they persisted in asking Him, He straightened up, and said to them, "He who is without sin among you, let him be the first to throw a stone at her."

The Law condemns. Everyone is in the same boat here. You are either the one that comes to condemn, or the one that comes condemned. Both need grace. Both needs saving grace, because both are sinful.

We have to drop our stones. It doesn't mean we don't hold one another accountable. Jesus took the Law, and He made it even harder, because you must come to realize that you can't be good enough!

Matthew 5:27–28
27 "You have heard that it was said, 'YOU SHALL NOT COMMIT ADULTERY'; 28 but I say to you that everyone who looks at a woman with lust for her has already committed adultery with her in his heart."

We should all be stoned. His words are compelling, because He, the Light of the world, speaks truth.

We do not need to be more convincing, but compelling. Speaking the truth, Jesus said, "He who is without sin among you, let him be the first to throw a stone at her."

Under the Law, we should be stoned for even looking at a woman or a man with lust. They were cut by the comment.

---

[6] Charles R. Swindoll, *Insights on John*, Swindoll's Living Insights New Testament Commentary (Grand Rapids, MI: Zondervan, 2014), 164.

John 8:7–9
7 "He who is without sin among you, let him be the first to throw a stone at her." 8 Again He stooped down and wrote on the ground. 9 When they heard it, they began to go out one by one, beginning with the older ones, and He was left alone, and the woman, where she was, in the center of the court.

To be compelling is to be truthful, and to be truthful is to bring about conviction. That is what the Holy Spirit does through His Word. Amidst all of this, there is a final characteristic we must look to as Christians.

WE MUST BE COMPASSIONATE CHRISTIANS

This last point is the reality of grace in compassion. It's important that, as Christians, we be compassionate and show compassion. We can certainly take this too far, but Jesus doesn't.

John 8:10–11
10 Straightening up, Jesus said to her, "Woman, where are they? Did no one condemn you?" 11 She said, "No one, Lord." And Jesus said, "I do not condemn you, either. Go. From now on sin no more."

Compassionate Christians must be gentle. Jesus is so gentle here—this is God in flesh. This is the holy, righteous, perfect, and sinless sacrifice who will pay for that sin, and your sin, and my sin.

John 8:10
10 "Woman, where are they? Did no one condemn you?"

In these words, Jesus highlights that they, too, need grace.

Compassionate Christians who are gentle with sinners know Christ and what it is to be forgiven. Jesus was perfect and never sinned, but He knew the struggle.

And Jesus said,

John 8:11
11 "I do not condemn you, either. Go. From now on sin no more."

It was a clean slate. Only God can forgive sins; God had not condemned her. She was still sinful, and so were they, but she was not condemned. She was forgiven.

He didn't just give her the OK to keep on sinning. Grace is never taken that way.

As Paul says,

Romans 6:1–2
1 What shall we say then? Are we to continue in sin so that grace may increase? 2 May it never be!

You need the same forgiveness she needed. You are either her or them; you're not Jesus. We all need grace upon grace.

We must be committed as Christians, be discerning to the world around us, compel people with the truth of God's Word, and hold fast to the compassion of Christ. This is our testimony.

Romans 8:1
1 Therefore there is now no condemnation for those who are in Christ Jesus.

She didn't seek Christ. She didn't deserve Christ. And she surely didn't earn her forgiveness.

We are all sinful and need the grace of Christ. Maybe you're reading, and you haven't lived a life that is honoring to God. Maybe you're like the woman caught in her sin. The call for you as you read this book is to stop right now and receive the forgiveness that Christ offers you personally—to believe the gospel, be saved, and go and sin no more.

CHAPTER 12

JESUS, THE LIGHT OF THE WORLD
John 8:12–20

There is a story that during the Vietnam War, there was a combat chopper radioed in one night to accomplish a top-secret mission. This mission would require the pilot to fly in total darkness, totally by his instruments.

Hovering above a jungle under heavy cloud cover and complete darkness, he radioed to his man on the ground and said, "What can you give me so that we can see you?"

The man did not even have a flashlight down below, making things very difficult, because the landing had to be precise. With such a small margin of error in the middle of the jungle, five feet to the left or right could crash the chopper and kill the entire team.

Finally, the man on the ground said, "I have a Zippo!" He said, "Light it and hold it up, so that we can see where you are and determine where to land."

So there, in the middle of the jungles of Southeast Asia, on this top-secret mission, the pilot landed and rescued the teammate because of a Zippo lighter that pierced the total, absolute darkness around.

When things are dark and you are walking around blinded by the darkness of this world, you can't see anything. You can't seem to land. You can't be saved. You can't even help save anyone else. You are simply crippled by the darkness. It's important to understand that when things are dark, it only takes a little light to pierce the darkness.

Jesus is making the claim that He is the Light when He says, "'I am the Light of the world'" (John 8:12).

In this chapter, as we consider John 8:12–20, there are four observations that will help us see that Christ is indeed the Light of the world: first, the claim of Christ; second, the criticism of Christ; third, the clarification of Christ; and finally, the conclusion of Christ.

Jesus has spoken in John 7:37–38, right at the perfect time when the priest would pour out the water in celebration. Jesus wanted to make a point in connection with God's Old Testament provision of water during the wilderness wandering. So, right as they were pouring out this water, it says that,

John 7:37–38
37 Jesus stood and cried out, saying, "If anyone is thirsty, let him come to Me and drink. 38 He who believes in Me, as the Scripture said, 'From his innermost being will flow rivers of living water.'"

The imagery is shocking. The point is taken. The idea is communicated. The promise is given. Just like God provided water for the survival of those in the wilderness wanderings, so now Jesus is the answer to our eternal salvation. He is our living water. And if you drink from Him, you will never thirst again (as Jesus says to the woman at the well in John 4:14).

And then, sandwiched between this and the account of living water, Jesus forgives an adulterous woman. The scribes and the Pharisees had brought this woman out to stone her before Christ. They tried to trick Jesus, but Jesus, being full deity, sees, knows, and understands their hearts and intentions, so He teaches them a lesson when He responds,

John 8:7
7 "He who is without sin among you, let him be the first to throw a stone at her."

They all walk away, and He says to her,

John 8:11
11 "I do not condemn you, either. Go. From now on sin no more."

His shocking imagery and stunning grace and forgiveness stand out. And now, we find ourselves here in John 8:12.

Jesus is at the temple. He is about to speak and teach again. He is about to take advantage of Old Testament imagery once again, like He did while the priest poured out the water in chapter 7. We know that He is there at the treasury.

John 8:20
20 These words He spoke in the treasury, as He taught in the temple;

I believe that He is there at the Feast of the Tabernacles. It's the final day, and while this celebration had its water ritual, there was another symbol, which was offered at night as the symbol of light. This was a celebration that would, "prompt memories of the pillars of cloud by day and fire by night, by which God himself lead His chosen people in their journey."[1]

The psalmist had taught that the Lord is my light.

Psalm 27:1
1 The LORD is my light and my salvation; Whom shall I fear? The LORD is the defense of my life; Whom shall I dread?

The Old Testament again points to the fact that Messiah would be the light to the nations.

Isaiah 42:6
6 "I am the LORD, I have called you in righteousness, I will also hold you by the hand and watch over you, And I will appoint you as a covenant to the people, As a light to the nations,"

Isaiah 49:6
6 He says, "It is too small a thing that You should be My Servant To raise up the tribes of Jacob and to restore the preserved ones of Israel; I will also make You a light of the nations So that My salvation may reach to the end of the earth."

This celebration of light pointed to the coming of Messiah. That's the context of what's happening here on the last day of the Feast of Tabernacles as the lights are going out.

There in the treasury, where the temple taxes were paid, there would have been four golden lamps that were lit at night, which would have been followed by great rejoicing. And on the last day, they are about to put them out.

It's here that we first see the claim of Christ.

---

[1] Bruce Milne, *The Message of John* (Westmont, IL: InterVarsity Press, 1993), 127.

THE CLAIM OF CHRIST

The imagery of God guiding His people in the wilderness unto salvation becomes so much more shocking. We see the picture of what Christ was claiming.

John 8:12
12 Then Jesus again spoke to them, saying, "I am the Light of the world;"

It was a cosmic claim. Jesus identifies Himself the same way that God identified Himself to Moses on the eve of the Exodus.

Exodus 3:14
14 God said to Moses, "I AM WHO I AM."

"I am God," is His claim—a claim the New Testament continually defends.

1 John 1:5
5 This is the message we have heard from Him and announce to you, that God is Light, and in Him there is no darkness at all.

Who is Light? God is Light. Jesus says, "I am the Light of the world" (John 8:12).

This is the second of seven major "I am" statements. The first time was Jesus' claim in John 6:35, when He said,

John 6:35
35 "I am the bread of life;"

His claim is that He is God. And in John 1:1, we are reminded right out of the gate,

John 1:1
1 In the beginning was the Word, and the Word was with God, and the Word was God.

That's the picture of what Christ is claiming, but we also see the promise of what Christ is claiming.

He says here, in the second part of John 8:12,

John 8:12
12 "he who follows Me will not walk in the darkness, but will have the Light of life."

This, my friends, is a promise unto spiritual life. This passage assumes that without following Christ, the Light of the world, the Son of God, you will wander aimlessly through life, walking in the darkness of your sins.

The Bible is clear that the wages of sin is death (Rom 6:23), and in Isaiah 59:2, it states,

Isaiah 59:2
2 But your iniquities have made a separation between you and your God, And your sins have hidden His face from you so that He does not hear.

If you are separated from God, you are wandering around aimlessly in the darkness. Without Christ, there is no light. He is the Light of the world.

And the promise is that,

John 8:12
12 "he who follows Me will not walk in the darkness, but will have the Light of life."

The claim prompts the question: Do you believe Christ? Because we must believe and follow the Light of the world, Jesus Christ, if we want eternal life.

THE CRITICISM OF CHRIST

Here, their criticism of the claims of Christ is plainly seen.

The text reads,

John 8:13
13 So the Pharisees said to Him, "You are testifying about Yourself; Your testimony is not true."

First, they are probably trying to take the words of Jesus hostage from what He spoke in John 5:30–31, when He said,

John 5:30–31
30 "I can do nothing by Myself; I judge only as I hear. And My judgment is just, because I do not seek My own will, but the will of Him who sent Me. 31 If I testify about Myself, My testimony is not valid."

That is the argument.

John 8:13
13 So the Pharisees said to Him, "You are testifying about Yourself; Your testimony is not true."

The Old Testament Law required every legal matter to be established by the testimony of two more witnesses (Deut 17:6, Num 35:30). Here, Christ is making a claim. He is establishing a testimony, but they are criticizing Him by saying that He is a liar. They're saying, "It's not true because, Jesus, You are testifying about Yourself." So, they are criticizing this as a contradiction.

People will criticize Christ with what they can come up with. People will simply make excuses and dig up whatever they can find to justify their own lifestyles while walking in the darkness, rather than turning to Christ, the Light of the world.

Why is that?

John 3:19–20
19 "This is the judgment, that the Light has come into the world, but men loved the darkness rather than the Light, because their deeds were evil. 20 For everyone who does evil hates the Light, and does not come to the Light for fear that his deeds will be exposed."

People love their sin. They are enticed by their own lust.

James 1:14–15
14 But each one is tempted when he is carried away and enticed by his own lust. 15 Then when lust has conceived, it gives birth to sin; and when sin is accomplished, it brings forth death.

The wages of sin is death (Rom 6:23). These people criticized the so-called contradiction, but they also criticized the truthfulness of God.

John 8:13
13 "Your testimony is not true."

God is truth. In Him is no lie. And what they have done is call God a liar. When you reject God the Holy Spirit, by rejecting God the Son, you reject God the Father, and you call God a liar.

Look at 1 John 5:10.

1 John 5:10
10 The one who believes in the Son of God has the testimony in himself; the one who does not believe God has made Him a liar, because he has not believed in the testimony that God has given concerning His Son.

We also see in,

Numbers 23:19
19 "God is not a man, that He should lie, Nor a son of man, that He should repent; Has He said, and will He not do it? Or has He spoken, and will He not make it good?"

What we see is their criticism of Christ and their disbelief in Jesus. The lesson here is simple: don't be like them. Don't reject God and make Him out to be a liar, lest you walk in darkness, aimlessly unto eternal punishment.

THE CLARIFICIATION OF CHRIST

Here, Christ is about to defend His claim.

John 8:12
12 "I am the Light of the world; he who follows Me will not walk in the darkness, but will have the Light of life."

The defense Christ gives for His claims is that He is the Light of the world, that He is God, and that He is not violating Old Testament Law by giving testimony of Himself. He clarifies, saying,

John 8:14–18
14 Jesus answered and said to them, "Even if I testify about Myself, My testimony is true, for I know where I came from and where I am going; but you do not know where I come from or where I am going. 15 You judge according to the flesh; I am not judging anyone. 16 But even if I do judge, My judgment is true; for I am not alone in it, but I and the Father who sent Me. 17 Even in your law it has been written that the testimony of two men is true. 18 I am He who testifies about Myself, and the Father who sent Me testifies about Me."

First, they have no clue who Jesus is. If they did, they would understand that you can't divide Christ. Jesus explains,

John 8:14
14 "Even if I testify about Myself, My testimony is true,"

How is that substantial evidence? Because He is God. Jesus has claimed to be God, and He is God. He is fully God and fully man. Jesus is deity, and God can't lie.

Romans 3:4
4 let God be found true, though every man be found a liar,

But not God. Therefore, whatever proceeds out of the mouth of Christ, is as if God Himself is speaking.

John 12:49
49 "For I did not speak on My own initiative, but the Father Himself who sent Me has given Me a commandment as to what to say and what to speak."

That's not enough evidence.

Deuteronomy 18:18
18 "I will raise up for them a prophet like you from among their brothers. I will put My words in his mouth, and he will tell them everything I command him."

Go back to John 5.

John 5:19

19 Therefore Jesus answered and was saying to them, "Truly, truly, I say to you, the Son can do nothing of Himself, unless it is something He sees the Father doing; for whatever the Father does, these things the Son also does in like manner."

Christ only speaks that which the Father speaks. Why? Because you can't divide Christ.

In John 16:12–15, Jesus said,

John 16:12–15
12 "I have many more things to say to you, but you cannot bear them now. 13 But when He, the Spirit of truth, comes, He will guide you into all the truth; for He will not speak on His own initiative, but whatever He hears, He will speak; and He will disclose to you what is to come. 14 He will glorify Me, for He will take of Mine and will disclose it to you. 15 All things that the Father has are Mine; therefore I said that He takes of Mine and will disclose it to you."

You can't separate Christ from the Trinity. You have God the Father, God the Son, and God the Holy Spirit, and here you see their connectivity. What He said may not be enough to stand in a court of law without two witnesses, but that doesn't make His claim untrue.

He goes even deeper, saying,

John 8:14

14 "for I know where I came from and where I am going; but you do not know where I come from or where I am going."

In chapter 1, John gives us a clear picture of where Christ came from.

John 1:1–3
1 In the beginning was the Word, and the Word was with God, and the Word was God. 2 He was in the beginning with God. 3 All things came into being through Him, and apart from Him nothing came into being that has come into being.

Jesus is saying that they don't know anything. They don't even know where He is from or where He is going. He does, and therefore, what He says is truth.

What Christ has given here really confirms that what He has said can't be deemed false just because there isn't another witness. It's truth without a witness.

Jesus says,

John 8:15

15 "You judge according to the flesh; I am not judging anyone."

The message is clear: your judgement is based on appearances, but you can't even get that right, because you love your sin so much. If you did judge based on appearances, you should believe because of the works He did.

John 8:16–18

16 "But even if I do judge, My judgment is true; for I am not alone in it, but I and the Father who sent Me. 17 Even in your law it has been written that the testimony of two men is true. 18 I am He who testifies about Myself, and the Father who sent Me testifies about Me."

The unity with the Father is key. The triune God makes the claim. He is the one that testifies, and no human witness can authenticate a divine relationship.

Job 38:4
4 "Where were you when I laid the foundation of the earth? Tell Me, if you have understanding,"

Jesus is saying, "I and the Father testify to My truth."

THE CONCLUSION OF CHRIST

It all comes down to one conclusion. Their unbelief is now not only internal, but external. They have taken a stance yet again.

John 8:19a

19a So they were saying to Him, "Where is Your Father?"

And the one sad conclusion is the final statement that Jesus makes.

John 8:19
19 Jesus answered, "You know neither Me nor My Father; if you knew Me, you would know My Father also."

The belief that they knew the Father of Jesus proves their ignorance.

Matthew 11:27
27 "All things have been handed over to Me by My Father; and no one knows the Son except the Father; nor does anyone know the Father except the Son, and anyone to whom the Son wills to reveal Him."

You can't know the Father unless the Son wills it. Therefore, if you reject Jesus, it's proof that you have no clue who the Father is. You can't say that you love God and reject Jesus, because Jesus says that He is the way unto the Father alone. He claims to be the Light of the world.

If you are saved by faith in Christ and are a follower of Christ, you have the Light of life.

Matthew 5:13–16
13 "You are the salt of the earth; but if the salt has become tasteless, how can it be made salty again? It is no longer good for anything, except to be thrown out and trampled under foot by men. 14 You are the light of the world. A city set on a hill cannot be hidden; 15 nor does anyone light a lamp and put it under a basket, but on the lampstand, and it gives light to all who are in the house. 16 Let your light shine before men in such a way that they may see your good works, and glorify your Father who is in heaven."

If you are reading this, and you haven't trusted in Christ alone, by grace alone, through faith alone, then you are wandering in the darkness of this world, and you are in desperate need of God's saving grace. You don't have a light to shine. You need Jesus today.

Christ has come into this world to seek and to save that which is lost. If you repent, believe the gospel, and follow Him, you will not walk in the darkness any longer.

CHAPTER 13

HOW NOT TO DIE IN YOUR SIN
John 8:21–30

The Merriam-Webster online dictionary defines the word, "remedy," as, "a medicine, application, or treatment that relieves or cures a disease."[1]

There are home remedies, herbal remedies, and natural remedies. Regardless of which category your remedy might fall into, all remedies have one thing in common: they are all trying to cure a problem.

It can be incredibly disappointing when the remedy fails to work. There is nothing worse than not being able to get rid of something that is bothering you. Having the right remedy is the key.

Receiving the right diagnosis to the problem is a crucial first step.

Months ago, when I did my chapter schedule, I titled this chapter, "How to Die in Your Sin." I wanted the title to be a little shocking. But as I worked through the text this week, I decided to entitle this chapter, "How NOT to Die in Your Sin."

Consider John 8:21–30. Jesus has quenched the people's thirst as He gives the living water of the Spirit (John 7:37). He gave His second "I am" statement (John 8:12). Throughout the Gospel of John, the focus has been on the One true remedy.

The proper remedy, the thrust of the text, the main point, is that, unless you believe that Jesus is the Christ, you will die in your sin. That's the remedy. It's not hidden. It's like a light shown in darkness; it is very clear, and Jesus is the only solution. You must believe, lest you die in your sin.

In this passage, we find four things the text drives us to see. First, we see the accusation of Christ. Second, we see the stipulation of Christ. Third, we see the explanation of Christ. And finally, we see the salvation of Christ.

---

[1] *Merriam Webster Online*, s.v. "Remedy, *n.*," accessed March 24, 2023, https://www.merriam-webster.com/dictionary/remedy/.

THE ACCUSATION OF CHRIST

Starting in verse 21, we read,

John 8:21–23
21 Then He said again to them, "I go away, and you will seek Me, and will die in your sin; where I am going, you cannot come." 22 So the Jews were saying, "Surely He will not kill Himself, will He, since He says, 'Where I am going, you cannot come'?" 23 And He was saying to them, "You are from below, I am from above; you are of this world, I am not of this world."

The remedy, the cure, the method through which Jesus desires these people to be saved, is through accusation. He accuses them of two different things. First, He explains their lostness to them. You can't know the good news until you first know the bad news. Good news isn't nearly as good when there isn't bad news. The bad news is what gives us the ability to see our need for the good news.

So, He reminds them,

John 8:21
21 Then He said again to them, "I go away, and you will seek Me, and will die in your sin; where I am going, you cannot come."

Notice the repetition in, "He said again to them." If you and I are going to be effective in reaching people with the hope of Jesus Christ, it's going to start with repetition, meaning that we will have to consistently, steadily, and repeatedly remind people of the bad news first. We have to remind people of their lostness. This was a method that Jesus adopted, if you remember, in John 7:33–34, when Jesus said to the people,

John 7:33–34
33 "For a little while longer I am with you, then I go to Him who sent Me. 34 You will seek Me, and will not find Me; and where I am, you cannot come."

This is the same grammatical structure here, as well as the same information. It's really the same accusations. Jesus is saying, "you're lost." The only difference here is that Jesus doesn't hold back. He outright condemns them.

John 8:21
21 Then He said again to them, "I go away, and you will seek Me, and will die in your sin; where I am going, you cannot come."

"You…will die in your sin;" is not an encouraging message, my friends. That is a message of damnation. If you and I are going to be faithful in giving the proper remedy to the world, then we must be willing to speak truth like Jesus spoke. We must be willing to tell people that, apart from Christ, they will die in their sin.

Here, they have Christ among them. The Messiah is right there, face-to-face with them. They have been seeking, they have been looking, they have been trying to find salvation and deliverance. And here, He kills their hope, saying, "Soon, I will go away, and when I go away, you will seek after Me, but will not find me! It will be too late, and you will die in your sin."

The accusations of Jesus are meant to bring about honest repentance. But even with that tough love, and even amidst accurate accusations, they fail to respond. This results in the same confusion in chapter 7 as there is in chapter 8.

In chapter 7, the Jews respond in confusion, saying,

John 7:35
35 "Where does this man intend to go that we will not find Him? He is not intending to go to the Dispersion among the Greeks, and teach the Greeks, is He?"

And here in John 8:22, the Jews also respond in confusion, saying,

John 8:22
22 So the Jews were saying, "Surely He will not kill Himself, will He, since He says, 'Where I am going, you cannot come'?"

They do not have a clue. They are lost.

The continual, repeated, long-echoing truth throughout the Word of God is this sobering fact: those who reject Christ will suffer the consequence of their sin and inherit separation from God eternally.

By rejecting Jesus as the life-giving water, by refusing the Light of the world and walking in darkness out of your own desire for sin, you will doom yourself to eternal destruction away from the presence of God.

If there was any doubt this is what Jesus was saying, Jesus makes sure that you and I get it. And so, after their little moment of confusion, He drops yet another striking accusation.

First, He explains to them their lostness. Second, He suggests that not only are they lost, but they are worldly.

John 8:23
23 And He was saying to them, "You are from below, I am from above; you are of this world, I am not of this world."

The way to not die in your sin is to believe the gospel of Jesus Christ. And the result of that believing is that you will be saved, not worldly.

Worldliness has kept many people out of the Kingdom of God, but the Word of God warns against this kind of behavior. As a matter of fact, John warns us of this in 1 John 2:15–17.

1 John 2:15–17
15 Do not love the world nor the things in the world. If anyone loves the world, the love of the Father is not in him. 16 For all that is in the world, the lust of the flesh and the lust of the eyes and the boastful pride of life, is not from the Father, but is from the world. 17 The world is passing away, and also its lusts; but the one who does the will of God lives forever.

Because they are lost, because they fail to believe that Jesus Christ is the Son of God, because they reject Jesus as Lord, they, and everyone else who rejects Him, are of this world according to the Bible. These people are not born from above; rather, their father is the devil. Jesus is very clear that these people who have rejected Him are not of Him. The remedy is to believe that Jesus Christ is Lord. Jesus accuses them of their lostness and of their worldliness.

THE STIPULATION OF CHRIST

Notice, if you will, how this next portion of Scripture begins in verse 24.

John 8:24
24 "Therefore I said to you that you will die in your sins; for unless you believe that I am He, you will die in your sins."

He starts out with the word, "therefore," and when we see the word, "therefore," we should always ask the question, "What is 'therefore' there for?" It points us back to what He has already said. He has given us the reason. He has given clarity. He has pointed out their faults.

John 8:24
24 "Therefore I said to you that you will die in your sins;"

The remedy for not dying in your sins is clear.

There are those who practice self-righteousness and worldliness. There are those who fail to believe. There are those who claim to be of Christ, yet walk in sin daily. There are those who claim to be saved, born-again believers, yet love their stuff, their toys, their children, their work, and their lives more than they love Jesus.

We are warned of this in Scripture.

Matthew 7:16–23
16 "You will know them by their fruits. Grapes are not gathered from thorn bushes nor figs from thistles, are they? 17 So every good tree bears good fruit, but the bad tree bears bad fruit. 18 A good tree cannot produce bad fruit, nor can a bad tree produce good fruit. 19 Every tree that does not bear good fruit is cut down and thrown into the fire. 20 So then, you will know them by their fruits. 21 Not everyone who says to Me, 'Lord, Lord,' will enter the kingdom of heaven, but he who does the will of My Father who is in heaven will enter. 22 Many will say to Me on that day, 'Lord, Lord, did we not prophesy in Your name, and in Your name cast out demons, and in Your name perform many miracles?' 23 And then I will declare to them, 'I never knew you; DEPART FROM ME, YOU WHO PRACTICE LAWLESSNESS.'"

Because of what you do, because of who you are, and because you reject Christ by your actions, Jesus says,

John 8:24a
24 "Therefore I said to you that you will die in your sins;"

So, Jesus has just caused some tension among those listening, and He has been very clear for His reasoning. Yet, He is now about to give some stipulations.

John 8:24
24 "Therefore I said to you that you will die in your sins; for unless you believe that I am He, you will die in your sins."

You see the escape route Christ has provided. You see the conditions, terms, and prerequisite He has given. That is grace.

Everyone who goes to Hell goes because they deserve it, and everyone who goes to Heaven does not deserve it. Hell is the very justice of God, and Heaven is the very grace of God.

You want to know the remedy?

John 8:24b
24 "for unless you believe that I am He, you will die in your sins."

What do you believe about Christ? Because Jesus says here, "Ego eimi" (ἐγώ εἰμί), which is, "I am." In the Greek, the pronoun "he" doesn't exist. Unless you believe that "I am," He says that you will die in your sins. It's a full claim to His deity, that He is indeed God in flesh.

Exodus 3:13–14 reminds us of this truth. This claim He is making becomes clear.

Exodus 3:13–14
13 Then Moses said to God, "Behold, I am going to the sons of Israel, and I will say to them, 'The God of your fathers has sent me to you.' Now they may say to me, 'What is His name?' What shall I say to them?" 14 God said to Moses, "I AM WHO I AM"; and He said, "Thus you shall say to the sons of Israel, 'I AM has sent me to you.'"

It's the same word structure.

John 8:24
24 "for unless you believe that I am He, you will die in your sins."

How not to die in your sins is to believe that He is God. If you believe that He is God and that God has paid for your sins, then you are not your own. You are a slave to Christ. No works, no efforts, no walk, no prayer, no human ability, can change the hearts of men. But let me say this: no changed man will be without works. No changed man will be without efforts. No changed man will be without prayer. No changed man will be without a fire for the things of God.

A sure method to die in sin is to not believe (or to pretend to believe). We are willing to do whatever it takes to serve what our God, or god, really is. We will spend our money on it. We will spend our time on it. We will spend our energy on it. We will sacrifice our family on the altar of it. We will risk our lives for it. That which consumes our minds, our hearts, and our desires is our God—or god. We need this reminder from Exodus.

Exodus 20:2–6
2 "I am the LORD your God, who brought you out of the land of Egypt, out of the house of slavery. 3 You shall have no other gods before Me. 4 You shall not make for yourself an idol, or any likeness of what is in heaven above or on the earth beneath or in the water under the earth. 5 You shall not worship them or serve them; for I, the LORD your God, am a jealous God, visiting the iniquity of the fathers on the children, on the third and the fourth generations of those who hate Me, 6 but showing lovingkindness to thousands, to those who love Me and keep My commandments."

Christ is clear. God is clear. The Holy Spirit is clear. This is the stipulation.

John 8:24
24 "for unless you believe that I am He, you will die in your sins."

It's a great reminder.

Exodus 20:3
3 "You shall have no other gods before Me."

How does that look in your life? What have you put first in your life? What is it that you have believed on?

John 14:6
6 Jesus said to him, "I am the way, and the truth, and the life; no one comes to the Father but through Me."

THE EXPLANATION OF CHRIST

Over the next five verses, Jesus is going to take the time to explain His meaning to these people. They are confused in verse 22. They are confused in verse 25, and they are confused in verse 27.

They ask Jesus a question in response to His stipulation, "for unless you believe that I am He, you will die in your sins."

John 8:25
25 So they were saying to Him, "Who are You?"

They just don't get it. They're saying, "So, who is it again that You say you are?" After all they have seen (the miracles, the signs, and the wonders), they still ask, "Who are You."

John 8:25
25 Jesus said to them, "What have I been saying to you from the beginning?"

The NASB translates this as a question, which means Jesus would be answering their question with a question. However, His is a question of affirmation and of explanation.

"What have I been saying to you from the beginning?" Jesus is saying, "I AM who I have been telling you over, and over, and over from the very beginning. I have been showing you in my Christological functions that I and the Father are one."

Lest they forget, Jesus says,

John 8:26
26 "I have many things to speak and to judge concerning you, but He who sent Me is true; and the things which I heard from Him, these I speak to the world."

But,

John 8:27
27 They did not realize that He had been speaking to them about the Father.

You can plead "fool," and you can play ignorant. But, if you want the proper remedy, Jesus says, "I am He, and You must believe that I am He, lest you die in your sin." And so, to respond to their confusion once again,

John 8:28
28 So Jesus said, "When you lift up the Son of Man, then you will know that I am He,"

He is saying, "You can claim I'll kill Myself, but you will lift Me up. I will die by My own will, but you will be the ones crucifying Me, not Myself. I will willingly lay down My life, but you will lift the Son of Man up."

Just like Moses in the wilderness, just like it was God then, it's God now.

John 8:28–29
28 "and I do nothing on My own initiative, but I speak these things as the Father taught Me. 29 And He who sent Me is with Me; He has not left Me alone, for I always do the things that are pleasing to Him."

He has just explained to them who He is and how He is connected to the Father so clearly. The unwillingness to hear and the blindness to see were powerful tools of the enemy in these men's lives.

THE SALVATION OF CHRIST

As always, Jesus is reaching people with salvation. He starts out with the accusation (their sin, their wickedness, and their separation). Then He gives a stipulation (the proper remedy). He continues again to explain who He is and how He, and the Father, and the Spirit are so connected. As a result, we see lives changed, and we see the Work of God in salvation. The text reads,

John 8:30
30 As He spoke these things, many came to believe in Him.

This wasn't a Pentecost conversion, where more than 3,000 come to faith, but there were some (many) who believed in Him.

God is all about saving the souls of those who would take hold of the proper remedy, place their faith in Jesus Christ for salvation, and be saved.

They came to believe, but it wasn't because of any thing they had done. It was a mighty work of God opening the eyes of the blind and giving them eyes to see. The text says many came to believe—not all, but many. Not everyone you witness to in life will be saved, but when they are given eyes to see and respond to that grace, you can know it is a work of God.

It won't be a life of simple confession (as we will see in the next chapter), but this is where it starts. True conversion is of God, and God changes the hearts of men and women. Those changed hearts grow in the Lord, and they become servants of the King, so that in the end, they can hear, "Well done, My good and faithful servant."

How to not die in your sin is to believe on the Lord Jesus Christ and be saved. What is stopping you today? You can start your life over today, right now, by trusting in Him. By taking hold of the proper cure, the right remedy unto salvation from above, you can be a child of God.

CHAPTER 14

THE MARKS OF TRUE FREEDOM
John 8:31–36

In Chuck Swindoll's book, *The Grace Awakening*,[1] he tells a story of one of the bloodiest wars in American history. It was a story of the time. A president had been assassinated. An amendment to the Constitution had been signed into law. Formerly enslaved men, women, and children were legally emancipated, released, and set free. They were unbound, and yet many, despite all of that, continued living in fear and in the captivity of slavery as though freedom had never happened. He said that in a context of hard-earned freedom, many of those emancipated slaves chose to remain slaves, rather than be set free.

There is, and will always be, a temptation to stay as you are, to not move, and to not choose to be changed. Maybe it comes from fear of what freedom will look like. Maybe it comes from worry that your career will be tanked, or that your marriage will be ruffled, or because you're scared that you will lose what you have worked so hard for up to this point in your life. Whatever the case, if we are not careful, we, like these folks, can choose to remain slaves. We would not be slaves in the same fashion, but rather, slaves to sin, instead of experiencing a true, biblical freedom.

In the Book of John, we have come to a place in which Jesus would like for us to move forward with purpose and to take the next steps in being faithful followers of Christ. True disciples of Christ. Disciples who really understand biblically what it is to be free.

Maybe you're reading today, and you have things that hold you down, or hold you back. Maybe you have things that keep you from experiencing the true freedom that has been offered. Or maybe you're like the Jewish people who are holding on to things that, in their minds, save them, but in reality, have no power. True freedom comes from Christ.

In John 8:31–36, Jesus has been teaching in the temple. There has been a crushing truth shared with the Jewish people, aimed especially at the leaders, and it applies even to us today.

---

[1] Charles Swindoll, *The Grace Awakening* (Nashville: Thomas Nelson, 2012),.94

John 8:24
24 "Therefore I said to you that you will die in your sins; for unless you believe that I am He, you will die in your sins."

That is a message of how to die in sin. By failing to believe that He is the Christ, the Son of the living God, and the I AM, you will die in your sins.

But even as hard of a message as that was for the Jewish people, there was a spark of hope. Verse 30 tells us that there were a few who came to believe in Him.

John 8:30
30 As He spoke these things, many came to believe in Him.

We don't know how many. We don't know how true their belief was. We only see that, "many came to believe in Him."

And that is the context of verses 31–36. This, combined with verses 37–59, form the entire pericope, meaning that whole section of text forms a coherent thought. Here in this chapter, there are three things to notice as we look at the marks of true freedom. First, see the qualifications of the believers. Second, the confusion of the Jews. And finally, the explanation of the Messiah.

THE QUALIFICATIONS OF THE BELIEVERS

It was just stated in verse 30 that,

John 8:30
30 As He spoke these things, many came to believe in Him.

We might think immediately that everyone who believed was saved. Why can that be problematic? Because throughout the Book of John, there were many places where people believed in Jesus, but there was no transformation and no heart change.

And so, Jesus, knowing this, said back in chapter 2,

John 2:23–25
23 Now when He was in Jerusalem at the Passover, during the feast, many believed in His name, observing His signs which He was doing. 24

But Jesus, on His part, was not entrusting Himself to them, for He knew all men, 25 and because He did not need anyone to testify concerning man, for He Himself knew what was in man.

They believed, but it wasn't a belief that seemingly led to salvation. We hear John 3:16 ringing in our ears as we consider this.

John 3:16
"For God so loved the world, that He gave His only begotten Son, that whoever believes in Him shall not perish, but have eternal life."

Is it enough to simply believe about Jesus Christ?

James 2:18–19
18 But someone may well say, "You have faith and I have works; show me your faith without the works, and I will show you my faith by my works." 19 You believe that God is one. You do well; the demons also believe, and shudder.

The demons believe in Jesus, but that doesn't make them saved. There can be a bit of confusion as to this whole idea. James alludes to it, but in verse 31, Jesus says,

John 8:31
31 So Jesus was saying to those Jews who had believed Him, "If you continue in My word, then you are truly disciples of Mine;"

Jesus is speaking to the Jews who had believed in Him from verse 30. Here, He gives them the first of two qualifiers that would allow you to test their faith or belief, and confirm that they are truly disciples of His.

Why would He do such a thing?

We can believe in just about anything, but that doesn't make it true. A man can believe that he is a woman, and our culture wants to believe that.

Likewise, we live in a day when many believe they are free in Christ. They trust that they are believers. They think they are followers of Christ. They hold to the idea that they have been redeemed, and that if Christ were to come back, or they were to go there, that they would be with Jesus.

So, what does Christ give us so that we can test our belief, so that we can be sure that we are truly His and truly free? What are the marks?

The first mark of true freedom (the first qualification of the Believer) is that the Believer must continue in His Word. The text says,

John 8:31
31 "If you continue in My word, then you are truly disciples of Mine;"

He says. Jesus says. Not me, not some preacher, not your systematic theology book, but rather Jesus says. Your Bible says, "If you continue in My Word, then you are truly disciples of Mine;" (emphasis added).

Notice that small word, the verb "eimi" ("are"), there in the text.

John 8:31
"If you continue in My word, then you ARE truly disciples of Mine;"
(emphasis added)

You aren't *becoming*. It doesn't say, "will become." Rather, it says, "you are," and you are only *if*. "*If* you continue in My word, *then* you are," (emphasis mine).

The heartbeat of your faith, the life of the walk, and the purity of your profession of Christ, is your ongoing progression in word and in deed. Scripture repeatedly affirms that those who have been saved will obey Christ. The theological term is, "the perseverance of the saints." It means to be steadfast and to continue.

Matthew 12:50
50 "For whoever does the will of My Father who is in heaven, he is My brother and sister and mother."

And in 1 John 5:3, it says,

1 John 5:3
3 For this is the love of God, that we keep His commandments; and His commandments are not burdensome.

They are not burdensome, because the believers know that their works don't save them. Rather, they are a by-product of what God has done in their hearts. That is why James said earlier,

James 2:18
18 "You have faith and I have works; show me your faith without the works, and I will show you my faith by my works."

James is saying, "You talk the talk, and I talk the walk."

In James 1:22, he says,

James 1:22
22 But prove yourselves doers of the word, and not merely hearers who delude themselves.

Transformation, salvation, and redemption all result in a continuing direction. On the flip side, we have seen those who have made professions of faith, but have failed to continue. Remember, it's not about perfection; it's about direction. Perfection in that Christ has made you perfect and righteous in the eyes of God (2 Cor 5:21), but that is positional sanctification. Here we are dealing with progressive sanctification, the ongoing act of becoming more and more like Christ, living out in deed the Christian walk.

I'm always reminded of the unforgettable story of Great Britain's 400-meter runner, Derek Redmond, whose hamstring snapped during his event. However, he was determined to finish the race at the Barcelona 1992 Olympic Games. Under the help of his father, he crossed the finish line.

Your God hasn't called you to do it on your own. He has given you the Helper, the Holy Spirit. Derek didn't win the race, but He finished the race. He kept his eye on the Prize and with the help of the father He crossed the finish line.

John 8:31
"If you continue in My word, then you are truly disciples of Mine;"

Faith and obedience in the process. This is not like what we find in that long chapter of John 6, with the culmination of the departure of many disciples.

John 6:66
66 As a result of this many of His disciples withdrew and were not walking with Him anymore.

The proof of our salvation isn't that one time you prayed a prayer or walked an aisle. The proof of your salvation is that you continue walking with Him.

That was the first mark of true freedom, that the believer must continue in His Word. The second of the two qualifiers of the believer is that the believer must come to know the truth.

John 8:31–32
31 So Jesus was saying to those Jews who had believed Him, "If you continue in My word, then you are truly disciples of Mine; 32 and you will know the truth, and the truth will make you free."

The mystery of the gospel is no longer a mystery for those who have believed. When you place your faith in Christ and believe on Him, you are indwelt with the Spirit of God. Therefore, because you are a true believer, you have been given a Helper, the Holy Spirit.

Jesus says in John 14:15–17,

John 14:15–17
15 "If you love Me, you will keep My commandments. 16 I will ask the Father, and He will give you another Helper, that He may be with you forever; 17 that is the Spirit of truth, whom the world cannot receive, because it does not see Him or know Him, but you know Him because He abides with you and will be in you."

True belief is marked by progress in the Word and by your knowledge of the truth. Not that you know everything, but that you learn as you grow in your walk with Christ, because the Holy Spirit is your teacher.

John 14:25–26
25 "These things I have spoken to you while abiding with you. 26 But the Helper, the Holy Spirit, whom the Father will send in My name, He will teach you all things, and bring to your remembrance all that I said to you."

It's the blessing of being in Christ, indwelt with the Spirit of God. Scripture is truth, and that is why Jesus can ask in the high priestly prayer in John 17:17.

John 17:17
17 "Sanctify them in the truth; Your word is truth."

Christ points to the fact that truly free people, true disciples of Christ, are marked by continuing in His Word and knowing the truth.

In John 14:6, Jesus says,

John 14:6
6 "I am the way, and the truth, and the life;"

And when you know the truth,

John 8:31–32
31 "If you continue in My word, then you are truly disciples of Mine; 32 and you will know the truth, and the truth will make you free."

Jesus Christ is the only one who can truly make you free. Have you been made free? Have you been continuing in His Word? Have you been growing in your knowledge of the truth? Because true freedom, saving grace, is marked by spiritual growth. This is because He who began a good work in you will finish it.

THE CONFUSION OF THE JEWS

The confusion that we find here is a confusion of what saves. It's a misunderstanding of position, and so, in response to verses 31 and 32, the Jews fire back.

John 8:33
33 They answered Him, "We are Abraham's descendants and have never yet been enslaved to anyone; how is it that You say, 'You will become free'?"

There needs to be some careful observations here, beginning first with who is speaking. The verse starts with, "They answered Him." And so, who is "they" referring to?

We might say it's obvious who the 'they' is, if He is indeed speaking to those Jews who 'came to believe in Him,' in verse 30. Then it would seem that, when the text says, "they," it's referring to those Jews who had believed.

But listen clearly. What is being said isn't being said of saved people. We know that because of what we find in verses 31–59, the whole pericope this text falls within. As a matter of fact, Jesus points out several areas that point to them really being lost.

John 8:34
34 Jesus answered them, "Truly, truly, I say to you, everyone who commits sin is the slave of sin."

He points out that they are slaves to sin in verse 42, when He states their lack of love for Him proves their lack of love for the Father.

John 8:42
42 Jesus said to them, "If God were your Father, you would love Me,"

This points to the idea that they didn't love Him; therefore, God wasn't their Father.

John 8:44
44 "You are of your father the devil,"

Doesn't that seem to assume that the people verse 33 refers to are lost?

But what happened in verses 30–32? The text says they believed in Him. He even went into teaching them the test, the qualification of being believers.

It follows that there were some who were saved. There were some who believed in Him. Verse 30 says that. But maybe there were some that, like before, said they believed, but when the rubber hit the road, they really only had a profession of faith.

The word, "they," in verse 33, then points to those moving forward in the passage who failed the test and didn't have the qualification. The reason for it was a misunderstanding of position. Those Jews were confused.

John 8:33

33 They answered Him, "We are Abraham's descendants and have never yet been enslaved to anyone; how is it that You say, 'You will become free'?"

They think that their connection to Abraham means they are safe. They think that they are the chosen race of God, and therefore, they are deemed to be free. That's the first reality that isn't clicking with them. What they are saying is, "Nationally, we are free."
Make this note: true freedom always comes from the correct source. We have already been given that source, and that is, and will always be, from Jesus Christ.

Isn't it interesting when people say they are Christians because of something they have done? Or that their family has done? Or because they are part of a religious group? It's false hope. Nothing, no one, not anything in your ability, nor in its own ability, can make you free like Christ makes one free.

Don't be deluded by the watering down of the gospel. Salvation comes by hearing the Word of God. When people are saved, when people are given new life in Christ, they will not be mistaken as to what saves them. Rather, they will say, "Jesus Christ is King. My life isn't my own, but rather, His, and I believe in salvation alone, by grace alone, through faith alone, which comes through Christ alone."

These people had been given freedom to worship their own God by the Romans. They thought that they were free and had never yet been enslaved to anyone, asking in verse *33, "[How] is it that You say, 'You will become free'?"*

They had really only known captivity. They had been subject to Assyria, Babylon, Persia, Greece, and now Rome.

They aren't talking about being nationally enslaved, because that would simply be foolish. No, they thought that because they were the chosen people of God, that they had a free ticket into heaven, because they understood that the Abrahamic covenant made them the children of God.

True salvation, true biblical freedom, comes from the correct source, and that is Jesus.

Let us not be confused like them. Salvation is found in a personal relationship with Jesus Christ. You will stand before Jesus. You will give an account for your life and how you served Him. No one else will stand in for you, unless you believe that Jesus Christ is Lord and your only source for salvation.

The marks of true freedom are:

- Continuing in His Word
- Knowing the Word of God

We have seen the qualifications of the believers, the confusion of the Jews, and we also see the explanation of the Messiah.

THE EXPLANATION OF THE MESSIAH

Jesus is about to clear things up. No confusion here. First, Jesus is going to clear up that, while they might think that they are free and not enslaved, that they, like all, are enslaved and in need of freedom.

And so, in response to this unbelieving talk,

John 8:34
34 Jesus answered them, "Truly, truly, I say to you, everyone who commits sin is the slave of sin."

What has Jesus just done? He has simply said, "You're a slave still, and you're not free, because you are a slave to sin. As a matter fact, anyone that commits sin, is a slave of sin…

That word, "everyone," makes this a universal statement.

Romans 3:23
23 for all have sinned and fall short of the glory of God,

Romans 3:10
10 as it is written, "THERE IS NONE RIGHTEOUS, NOT EVEN ONE;"

Because we have all sinned, we have all been enslaved to it. We all need to be set free from the bondage of sin.

This is a call to repentance. God doesn't approve if you keep walking in sin. As a matter of fact, He will discipline you for it.

Hebrews 12:5–7
5 "MY SON, DO NOT REGARD LIGHTLY THE DISCIPLINE OF THE LORD, NOR FAINT WHEN YOU ARE REPROVED BY HIM; 6 FOR THOSE WHOM THE LORD LOVES HE DISCIPLINES, AND HE SCOURGES EVERY SON WHOM HE RECEIVES." 7 It is for discipline that you endure; God deals with you as with sons; for what son is there whom his father does not discipline?

Christ has not set you free in freedom to sin. May it never be. Be reminded of this great theological truth, the assurance of salvation.

John 8:35
35 "The slave does not remain in the house forever; the son does remain forever."

He who walks in sin is a slave to it, and therefore is a slave of it. And like the one in this passage, he doesn't remain in the house forever. Rather, he, the slave, takes no ownership and no sonship. He can be moved. He can be sold. He has no rights in that position.

But a son is one who has ownership. He is entitled to rights, benefits, and to the inheritance. He is not entitled because He has done anything, but because He was born into the family. He holds the position of son.

God has given His Son that you, like me, might have true freedom. When you become a son of God, you will remain forever. That is why He can say, starting in verse 31,

John 8:31–32
31 "If you continue in My word, then you are truly disciples of Mine; 32 and you will know the truth, and the truth will make you free."

Why? Because Jesus's conclusion, as He explains to those Jews (and us) what it is to be free, is,

John 8:36
36 "So if the Son makes you free, you will be free indeed."

Jesus is saying, "You will walk in my Word. You will know the truth, and the truth shall set you free. This is because you understand the correct source of freedom, and that is found in being a child of God."

We were all slaves to sin at one point in our lives. But there is a Man who fought for your spiritual freedom. There is a Man who fought the bloodiest war on earth. As a matter of fact, He shed His blood on Calvary. His name is Jesus Christ. He was assassinated by way of crucifixion, and that sacrifice grants anyone who would believe in Him, to be set free. It was hard-earned freedom that was offered by grace, but many walk around entrenched in the bondage of sin and separation as they choose to remain as slaves.

Choose this day whom you will serve, because "if the Son makes you free, you will be free indeed."

CHAPTER 15

MISTAKEN IDENTITY
John 8:37–47

I once heard a story that took place in one of the most intense burn seasons, where fires were raging out of control. A cameraman who desired to get some video shots of burning hillside in the valley, requested that the company allow him to charter a flight so he could get the video.

With his request approved, the news cameraman quickly used his cell phone to call the local airport to charter a flight. He was told a twin-engine plane would be waiting for him at the airport. Arriving at the airfield, he spotted a plane warming up outside a hanger. He jumped in with his bag, slammed the door shut, and shouted, "Let's go!"

The pilot taxied out, swung the plane into the wind, and took off. Once in the air, the cameraman instructed the pilot, "Fly over the valley, and make low passes so that I can get shots of the fires on the hillsides." "Why?" asked the pilot. "Because I'm a cameraman for the news station," he responded, "and I need to get some close-up shots." The pilot was strangely silent for a moment. Finally, he stammered, "So, what you're telling me, is that you're not my flight instructor?"

Mistaken identity can cause you major problems. The devil has no greater tool than mistaken identity.

In John, these Jews were blinded to their mistaken identity. And if you and I are not careful, we too, like them, can live out our lives here on this earth, with a form of mistaken identity.

In John 8:30, Jesus had been telling the Jewish people that He is the Light of the World and that He is the Great I AM. There was a list of negative points made throughout that portion of Scripture, but verse 30 says,

John 8:30
30 As He spoke these things, many came to believe in Him.

There were those who had trusted in Christ unto salvation, and there were those that also believed, but only with a John 2 kind of belief that wasn't transformational.

It was then that Jesus gave the marks of true freedom, stating,

John 8:31–32
31 "If you continue in My word, then you are truly disciples of Mine; 32 and you will know the truth, and the truth will make you free."

These two qualifications exposed those in the crowd who had not believed with a belief that resulted in salvation. It is the Son who brings about true, genuine salvation.

And He says,

John 8:36
36 "So if the Son makes you free, you will be free indeed."

They had claimed that they were descendants of Abraham, and they had confidence in their freedom because of that. But a mistaken idea of who you are in Christ will lead you to destruction.

This is the context for this text. There are three things here that will help you evaluate your identity in Christ. These are the tools, marks, or observations, Jesus used to point out the mistaken identity of the Jews. First, we see the correction of Christ. Second, we see the clarification of Christ. And finally, we see the conclusion of Christ.

THE CORRECTION OF CHRIST

Notice first that He confirms who they are before He begins correcting them.

John 8:37
37 "I know that you are Abraham's descendants;"

Remember in John 8:33, the Jews said,

John 8:33
33 "We are Abraham's descendants and have never yet been enslaved to anyone; how is it that You say, 'You will become free'?"

Jesus is confirming that they are truly Abraham's descendants. The Greek word σπέρμα that is used here, the same Greek word used in verse 33, is translated "descendants." Jesus confirms that they are in the line of Abraham. But notice what He says next.

John 8:37
37 "yet you seek to kill Me, because My word has no place in you."

He is saying, "You are indeed descendants, but you have a mistaken identity. You think that because you are descendants, you are delivered. You think that because you are relatives, you are redeemed; but your deeds don't match your reality."

If Jesus tells you that, "My word has no place in you," then you can count on the fact that you are indeed, not a true disciple of Christ, because He has already said,

John 8:31
31 "If you continue in My word, then you are truly disciples of Mine;"

He is saying, "While you are indeed descendants, your deeds confirm your mistaken identity."

Matthew 7:15–16
15 "Beware of false prophets. They come to you in sheep's clothing, but inwardly they are ravenous wolves. 16 By their fruit you will recognize them."

Jesus sees them for who they are. He realizes that they think they are something they are not, so He starts making comparisons to reveal their true identity. He starts to make corrections in their thinking. So, He says in John 8:38,

John 8:38
38 "I speak the things which I have seen with My Father; therefore you also do the things which you heard from your father."

He is saying something to them beneath the surface, without coming right out and saying it. He has just told them that His Father is different than their father. The translation makes the distinction using the capitalization of "the Father" of Jesus and their "father."

These Jews are only doing what they see and hear from their fathers.

Acts 7:51
51 "You men who are stiff-necked and uncircumcised in heart and ears are always resisting the Holy Spirit; you are doing just as your fathers did."

Therefore, Jesus says,

John 8:38
38 "I speak the things which I have seen with My Father; therefore you also do the things which you heard from your father."

And in verse 44, He will reveal who their father is, but it was years of their earthly fathers not working and serving the Father of Jesus, God.

And so, they pick up on what He is saying.

John 8:39
39 They answered and said to Him, "Abraham is our father."

Jesus corrects them.

John 8:39
39 Jesus said to them, "If you are Abraham's children, do the deeds of Abraham."

Notice it's no longer "descendants," but, "children." It's no longer "sperma," but now, it's τέκνα. It's the Greek word that means, "child."

Jesus isn't doubting that they are descendants, but He's clarifying that they are not children of Abraham. He has already said that their deeds confirm their mistaken identity.

John 8:39
39 "If you are Abraham's children, do the deeds of Abraham."

Abraham was a righteous man, and he listened to the words of God. But Jesus has already told them,

John 8:37
37 *"My word has no place in you."*

Jesus is telling them that they would do the deeds of Abraham if they were really his children.

John 8:40
40 *"But as it is, you are seeking to kill Me, a man who has told you the truth, which I heard from God; this Abraham did not do."*

Jesus has to correct their thinking, because their deeds are speaking much louder than their words.

If you're claiming that God is your Father, note that it's only by grace alone, through faith alone, in Christ alone, that you are truly a child of God.

Paul reminds us in Romans 9:6–8,

Romans 9:6–8
6 But it is not as though the word of God has failed. For they are not all Israel who are descended from Israel; 7 nor are they all children because they are Abraham's descendants, but: "THROUGH ISAAC YOUR DESCENDANTS WILL BE NAMED." 8 That is, it is not the children of the flesh who are children of God, but the children of the promise are regarded as descendants.

Being a descendant doesn't make one saved. Paul agrees with Jesus, when he says in Galatians,

Galatians 3:6–9
6 Even so Abraham BELIEVED GOD, AND IT WAS RECKONED TO HIM AS RIGHTEOUSNESS. 7 Therefore, be sure that it is those who are of faith who are sons of Abraham. 8 The Scripture, foreseeing that God would justify the Gentiles by faith, preached the gospel beforehand to Abraham, saying, "ALL THE NATIONS WILL BE BLESSED IN YOU." 9 So then those who are of faith are blessed with Abraham, the believer.

Jesus had to correct their thinking. It's only by faith in Christ that we can be called children of God.

THE CLARIFICATION OF CHRIST

In response to the fact of verse 40, He says,

John 8:41a
41 "You are doing the deeds of your father."

There it is once again, a distinction between the Father of Jesus and their father.

They make no long and drawn-out remarks. This whole section is really a one-sided conversation, but here,

John 8:41b
41 They said to Him, "We were not born of fornication; we have one Father: God."

Now they switched from their freedom in Abraham to the mistaken identity that somehow their Father is God.

Not everyone who says they are a Christian is a Christian. Ask the right questions, because they will come making the claim, but inwardly, they are wrong.

Jesus has to clear up the muddy water.

Yet they make a bold claim when they say, "We were not born of fornication; we have one Father: God."

Here is what they are saying: "Jesus, You claim that God is your Father, but you're a child born of fornication. We weren't."

And so,

John 8:42
42 Jesus said to them, "If God were your Father, you would love Me, for I proceeded forth and have come from God, for I have not even come on My own initiative, but He sent Me."

The mark of true identity is love for the Son. What Jesus is saying is, "Your lack of love for Me confirms your mistaken identity." Your lack of deeds and your lack of love are really like a double-sided coin. In John 14:15, Jesus says,

John 14:15
15 "If you love Me, you will keep My commandments."

Essentially, He is saying, "If God were truly your Father, then you would love Me." But Jesus clarifies that their lack of love for Jesus proves that God isn't their Father.

In verse 42, He is saying, "I come from God. It wasn't even my decision, nor by My own initiative, but God's."

John 3:16
16 "For God so loved the world,"

It doesn't stop there.

1 John 4:10
10 In this is love, not that we loved God, but that He loved us and sent His Son to be the propitiation for our sins.

And then, there is Romans 5:8.

Romans 5:8
8 But God demonstrates His own love toward us, in that while we were yet sinners, Christ died for us.

And there is Romans 8:32.

Romans 8:32
32 He who did not spare His own Son but gave Him up for us all, how will He not also, along with Him, freely give us all things?

Then, there is Romans 8:39.

Romans 8:39
39 neither height nor depth, nor anything else in all creation, will be able to separate us from the love of God that is in Christ Jesus our Lord.

It was, and has always been, the rescue plan of the almighty God.

Jesus is saying, "I am He, here to save your soul, but you don't love me "

And so, He says,

John 8:43a
43 "Why do you not understand what I am saying?"

And then He answers His own question.

John 8:43b
43 "It is because you cannot hear My word."

He is saying, "Because you cannot hear My word, which is the Father's word, your Father isn't God." In verse 44, Jesus goes on and clarifies this, saying,

John 8:44a
44 "You are of your father the devil,"

Looking back now, we can see that gap filled in, in verse 38, when Jesus says,

John 8:38
38 "I speak the things which I have seen with My Father; therefore you also do the things which you heard from your father (the devil)."

We can see that gap filled in verse 41, when Jesus says,

John 8:41a
41 "You are doing the deeds of your father (the devil)."

John 8:44a
44 "You are of your father the devil and you want to do the desires of your father."

And the results of that is that,

- You're a murderer.
- You don't stand in truth.
- You speak only lies.

John 8:44b
44 "He was a murderer from the beginning, and does not stand in the truth because there is no truth in him. Whenever he speaks a lie, he speaks from his own nature, for he is a liar and the father of lies."

There is nothing below the surface anymore. It's revealed. It's true that we all have to come to this place where we understand who we are, if we want to be saved. Who are you? Who is your Father?

THE CONCLUSION OF CHRIST

Every story has a conclusion. They have done as their father has done. They are who their father is. And their lack of hearing the truth confirms their mistaken identity.

John 8:45
45 "But because I speak the truth, you do not believe Me."

Jesus is saying, "You do the very opposite. You believe in lies. Your lack of ability to hear truth is a mark of false identity. You don't believe, because I speak truth, and you can only believe a lie."

Do you think that because you do good, you can make it? Do you think that because you're a descendant of some godly grandparent, some godly father, mother, brother, or sister, you will be saved? Do you think that because you hold the Law, you can be granted forgiveness?

If you could be saved by maintaining the Law, then Christ didn't need to die. Jesus adds,

John 8:46a
46 "Which one of you convicts Me of sin?"

None. Why?

2 Corinthians 5:21
21 He made Him who knew no sin to be sin on our behalf, so that we might become the righteousness of God in Him.

Jesus speaks only truth, and there is no sin in Him. He says,

John 8:46–47
46 "If I speak truth, why do you not believe Me? 47 He who is of God hears the words of God; for this reason you do not hear them, because you are not of God."

People aren't walking away from the faith. They were never of the faith; they didn't feel that drawing of the Holy Spirit if they rejected the call of God.

It's not a sanctification issue with people walking away. It's a salvation issue. It's the one who hears the words of God that is of God, and only God can give you ears to hear. No work, no method, no law, no trickery, no nothing, but God opening your ears to hear, giving you the ability to respond by faith to the gospel.

Anyone who places his or her trust in anything other than the Person and work of Jesus Christ alone for salvation is living a mistaken identity, and his or her father is not God. Salvation is by grace alone, through faith alone, in Christ alone. It's only then that you can be considered a child of God.

CHAPTER 16

THE DENIAL OF DEITY
John 8:48–59

"Scott Goodyear, speaking of race-car drivers who have been killed in crashes at the Indianapolis 500, said; 'You don't go look at where it happened. You don't watch the films of it on television. You don't deal with it. You pretend it never happened.' The Speedway operation itself encourages this approach. As soon as the track closes the day of an accident, a crew heads out to paint over the spot where the car hit the wall. Through the years, a driver has never been pronounced dead at the race track. A trip to the Indianapolis Motor Speedway Racing Museum, located inside the 2.5-mile oval, has no memorial to the 40 drivers who have lost their lives there. Nowhere is there even a mention."[1]

The denial doesn't delete the reality.

We have become really good at ignoring the facts. We have become professionals at hiding the truth. And we have treated God in the same manner.

In John 8:48–59, we find the culmination of the deity of Christ in this dialogue between the Jewish authorities and Jesus Christ Himself.

It hasn't been an easy process for these Jewish people. Jesus Christ has threatened their very integrity and self-esteem. As a result of this truth pouring down upon them, we find a special denial that causes a vitriol, a hatred, a bitterness, and a cruel response, as a result.

It doesn't matter how mad or how angry they might get. It doesn't matter how much they deny the reality that Jesus is the Christ, the Great I AM. They can deny it. They can pretend that it is not so. They can even try to destroy the truth of it, but its reality is so.

Notice in this text that we see the defamation of character, the distrust of the Jews, and the declaration of deity. These points help frame our passage.

---

[1] James Tilley, "Christ Is the Explanation of Existence," *Sermon Central*, December 10, 2009, accessed March 24, 2023, https://www.sermoncentral.com/sermons/christ-is-the-explanation-of-existence-james-tilley-sermon-on-faith-141950?page=1&wc=800.

THE DEFAMATION OF CHARACTER

It has been said, "When the debate is lost, slander becomes the tool of the losers." The Jews were certain that they were children of Abraham, but Jesus examined that claim based upon their actions, when He stated,

John 8:39–40
39 "If you are Abraham's children, do the deeds of Abraham. 40 But as it is, you are seeking to kill Me, a man who has told you the truth, which I heard from God; this Abraham did not do."

John 8:42
42 "If God were your Father, you would love Me,"

John 8:43–44
43 "Why do you not understand what I am saying? It is because you cannot hear My word. 44 You are of your father the devil, and you want to do the desires of your father. He was a murderer from the beginning, and does not stand in the truth because there is no truth in him. Whenever he speaks a lie, he speaks from his own nature, for he is a liar and the father of lies."

They respond to this claim of Christ, and this is the context for this passage of Scripture.

And so, the text says,

John 8:48
48The Jews answered and said to Him, "Do we not say rightly that You are a Samaritan and have a demon?"

They have just insulted Jesus. They are defaming the character of Christ. That's the easy thing to do when the debate is lost. They can't prove Jesus to be wrong. He is right, and slander thus becomes the tool. Insults rain down on Him, and vilification becomes their method. When their theological argument fails, Jesus' opponents turn to personal abuse.[2]

---

[2] D. A. Carson, *The Gospel According to John*, Pillar New Testament Commentary (Grand Rapids, MI: Eerdmans, 1991), 354.

By calling Jesus a "Samaritan," they are calling Him a heretic. These Jews despised the Samaritans as physical and spiritual half-breeds. The Samaritans were the descendants of Jews who had remained in the Northern Kingdom (Israel) after its fall and intermarried with pagans transplanted there by Assyrians.

In Ezra 4:1–3, when the Samaritans desired to help rebuild the temple after the exiles, the Jews said no, and they were highly insulted.

To call Jesus a "Samaritan" was to call Him a false teacher. Why? Remember the woman at the well, in John 4? If you recall the woman said,

John 4:19–20
19 "Sir, I perceive that You are a prophet. 20 Our fathers worshiped in this mountain, and you people say that in Jerusalem is the place where men ought to worship."

Every good Jew knew these Samaritans had bad theology. You can only worship God in Jerusalem in the temple. Therefore, if Jesus was a Samaritan, He, like them, was a false teacher, a fake, and a fraud.

Adding insult to insult, not only do they claim that He is a Samaritan, but also that He has a demon.

John 8:48b
48 *"Do we not say rightly that You are a Samaritan and have a demon?"*

This was a common insult for Jesus.

Mark 3:22
22 The scribes who came down from Jerusalem were saying, "He is possessed by Beelzebul," and "He casts out the demons by the ruler of the demons."

John 7:19–20
19 "Why do you seek to kill Me?" 20 The crowd answered, "You have a demon! Who seeks to kill You?"

This is a real problem. They are accusing Jesus, God in flesh, of having a demon. As a matter of fact, in Mark 3:30, just eight verses after they accuse him of being possessed by Beelzebul, we find,

Mark 3:28–30
28 "Truly I say to you, all sins shall be forgiven the sons of men, and whatever blasphemies they utter; 29 but whoever blasphemes against the Holy Spirit never has forgiveness, but is guilty of an eternal sin"— 30 because they were saying, "He has an unclean spirit."

This is sheer blasphemy. What we see is the defamation of character against the King of kings and Lord of lords.

How often do we question God's character in a similar way?

- "How can God be a good God and let bad things happen to good people?"
- "How can God allow a man to just walk into the church and shoot it up?"
- "God has just forgotten about me and my people!"
- "Obviously, God doesn't know what He is doing, does He?"
- "God doesn't care about me or my family, or He wouldn't let us go through this."

These Jews wanted to defame Christ when they couldn't have what they wanted. And that was the freedom to be their own god and decide what truth really was. They wanted to be the ones to tell God what's okay, what's sin, what's not sin, what's good, and what's evil.

Jesus responds to their accusations.

John 8:49–50
49 Jesus answered, "I do not have a demon; but I honor My Father, and you dishonor Me. 50 But I do not seek My glory; there is One who seeks and judges."

He turns it right back on them, essentially saying, "If I had a demon, I wouldn't honor God! But I do honor God." He says that in,

John 4:34
34 Jesus said to them, "My food is to do the will of Him who sent Me and to accomplish His work."

John 5:30
30 "I can do nothing on My own initiative. As I hear, I judge; and My judgment is just, because I do not seek My own will, but the will of Him who sent Me."

John 6:38,
38 "For I have come down from heaven, not to do My own will, but the will of Him who sent Me."

John 14:31
31 "I do exactly as the Father commanded Me."

John 15:10
10 "If you keep My commandments, you will abide in My love; just as I have kept My Father's commandments and abide in His love."

John 17:14
14 "I have given them Your word; and the world has hated them, because they are not of the world, even as I am not of the world."

John 5:19
19 "Truly, truly, I say to you, the Son can do nothing of Himself, unless it is something He sees the Father doing; for whatever the Father does, these things the Son also does in like manner."

The irony is that the people do not do the Father's deeds. This makes them a more fitting target of their own insult.

THE DISTRUST OF THE JEWS

He says,

John 8:51
51 "Truly, truly, I say to you, if anyone keeps My word he will never see death."

But do they buy it, or do they deny it? We are told in John 8:52–53 that,

John 8:52–53
52 The Jews said to Him, "Now we know that You have a demon. Abraham died, and the prophets also; and You say, 'If anyone keeps

177

My word, he will never taste of death.' 53 "Surely You are not greater than our father Abraham, who died? The prophets died too; whom do You make Yourself out to be?"

Their minds are focused on what is temporal. They are physically focused, and their logic is not biblical.

Remember John 8:47, when Jesus says,

John 8:47
47 "He who is of God hears the words of God; for this reason you do not hear them, because you are not of God."

They miss what He is saying, because they know not the One saying it.

They have distrusted, they do not believe, and they even go as far as to deny. But it's only if one keeps His Word that he will never taste death (John 8:52). The Bible says,

Acts 16:31
"Believe in the Lord Jesus, and you will be saved,"

You will gain understanding, and the things that you once denied, you will embrace and promote. They distrust Him because they are dead. They are not of God. They are lost and are not born again.

They were confused as to what Jesus is talking about, and so they ask in John 8:53,

John 8:53b
53 "whom do You make Yourself out to be?"

He is God. He is greater than Abraham. He is greater than the prophets. John the Baptist spoke of the prophets that spoke of Christ to come.

John 1:23
23 He said, "I am A VOICE OF ONE CRYING IN THE WILDERNESS, 'MAKE STRAIGHT THE WAY OF THE LORD,' as Isaiah the prophet said."

There was great distrust in the only One they could trust. Scripture says,

Jeremiah 17:9
9 "The heart is more deceitful than all else And is desperately sick; Who can understand it?"

Don't let your confusion give you confidence in the wrong thing. Jesus keeps explaining.

John 8:54–55
54 Jesus answered, "If I glorify Myself, My glory is nothing; it is My Father who glorifies Me, of whom you say, 'He is our God'; 55 and you have not come to know Him, but I know Him; and if I say that I do not know Him, I will be a liar like you, but I do know Him and keep His word."

Here we find again, the difference between lost and found, and the difference between saved and unsaved.

They didn't believe, so He leaves no rock unturned. They are liars and deniers, and while they think they keep His Word, they don't.

John 8:56–57
56 "Your father Abraham rejoiced to see My day, and he saw it and was glad." 57 So the Jews said to Him, "You are not yet fifty years old, and have You seen Abraham?"

They don't believe at all. So, they question Jesus, yet again. The gospel is what saves people, not having all the answers. They don't even really want the answers, in this case.

John 8:57
57 "You are not yet fifty years old, and have You seen Abraham?"

They are about to get an answer.

THE DECLARATION OF DEITY

Only God can answer, "Yes," to that question. Only a pre-existing Jesus can say, "Yes." And if Jesus is pre-existing, meaning that there is never a time in which He did not exist, then He is God.

The Bible you have before you teaches that truth from beginning to end.

Revelation 1:8
8 "I am the Alpha and the Omega," says the Lord God, "who is and who was and who is to come, the Almighty."

Later in the same chapter, under the same context, we read,

Revelation 1:17–18
17 When I saw Him, I fell at His feet like a dead man. And He placed His right hand on me, saying, "Do not be afraid; I am the first and the last, 18 and the living One; and I was dead, and behold, I am alive forevermore, and I have the keys of death and of Hades."

It is Christ who is the beginning and end; it's Jesus who embodies all deity.

Colossians 1:13–17
13 For He rescued us from the domain of darkness, and transferred us to the kingdom of His beloved Son, 14 in whom we have redemption, the forgiveness of sins. 15 He is the image of the invisible God, the firstborn of all creation. 16 For by Him all things were created, both in the heavens and on earth, visible and invisible, whether thrones or dominions or rulers or authorities—all things have been created through Him and for Him. 17 He is before all things, and in Him all things hold together.

Jesus has told the Jews that if they see Him, then they have seen the Father. So, when they, ask, "You are not yet fifty years old, and have You seen Abraham?" we read,

John 8:58
58 Jesus said to them, "Truly, truly, I say to you, before Abraham was born, I am."

It's the culmination of the deity of Christ. It is the climactic reply of this whole debate with the Jewish leaders, and it now comes to a close.

What He is saying is, "Before Abraham was ever born, I, Yahweh was there."[3] Jesus was around long before Abraham and long before the prophets, because He is God in flesh, and there is never a time in which Jesus Christ didn't exist.

---

[3] Grant Osborne, *John Verse by Verse* (Bellingham, WA: Lexham Press, 2018), 232.

And yet they reject Him. What we see is the denial of deity. We see blasphemy and rejection of God in flesh. You can respond as they did, or you can fall at the feet of the King of kings and Lord of Lords.

The text says,

John 8:59
59 Therefore they picked up stones to throw at Him, but Jesus hid Himself and went out of the temple.

They tried to kill Him. Why? Because He makes Himself out to be God. To reject Christ as being God is to blaspheme His name. Denial of the deity of Christ, rejecting Jesus as Messiah, as Lord, and as God in flesh, is to blaspheme against Him. If it were possible, those who reject Him would crucify Him all over again.

We must submit our lives to Christ for who He is, place our faith in who He is, and believe in who He is. He is God incarnate, God in flesh, God with us, so that we might never taste death.

Just because you don't look, doesn't mean God isn't there. Just because you don't read the Bible, or listen to a sermon, doesn't mean God isn't talking. Just because you don't deal with it, doesn't mean He won't deal with you.

Scripture would say you already know.

Romans 1:18–25
18 For the wrath of God is revealed from heaven against all ungodliness and unrighteousness of men, who by their unrighteousness suppress the truth. 19 For what can be known about God is plain to them, because God has shown it to them. 20 For his invisible attributes, namely, his eternal power and divine nature, have been clearly perceived, ever since the creation of the world, in the things that have been made. So they are without excuse. 21 For although they knew God, they did not honor him as God or give thanks to him, but they became futile in their thinking, and their foolish hearts were darkened. 22 Claiming to be wise, they became fools, 23 and exchanged the glory of the immortal God for images resembling mortal man and birds and animals and creeping things. 24 Therefore God gave them up in the lusts of their hearts to impurity, to the dishonoring of their bodies among themselves, 25

because they exchanged the truth about God for a lie and worshiped and served the creature rather than the Creator, who is blessed forever! Amen.

Today is the day of salvation. The denial of deity is to blaspheme the name of Christ. Believe that God became a man to live that perfect life, to take your place on the cross at Calvary. Believe the Gospel, so that you might live with Him forever in eternity.

ABOUT THE AUTHOR

Pastor Stuart Guthrie earned his undergraduate degree from Columbia International University in Columbia, South Carolina, and completed his Master's degree at Dallas Theological Seminary. Pastor Guthrie also holds a Doctorate of Ministry from The Master's Seminary. While he has served as Pastor/Teacher for well over a decade, his focus has been drawn continually to full-time ministry since his conversion. Pastor Guthrie began as the teaching pastor at Family Bible Fellowship in January 2017, and he has great hope to see how the Lord will use this local body of believers to accomplish His will in the Yemassee community and throughout the world.

Pastor Guthrie and his wife, Jennifer, reside in the Lowcountry of South Carolina with their seven children and share a passion to convey biblical truth, seeking to encourage and inform the promotion and health of the family, as determined through Scripture. Pastor Guthrie is committed to the exegetical preaching of the Word and to reaching the lost with the hope of Jesus Christ.

To contact Pastor Stuart Guthrie for speaking engagements, or for other books written by Pastor Guthrie, visit his website at https://www.stuartguthrie.com

Made in the USA
Columbia, SC
15 April 2023

3bafd02f-4c9b-42d6-982d-faec889aee0bR02